Far as the Curse Is Found

Far as the Curse Is Found

Searching for God in Infertility,
Miscarriage, and Stillbirth

ABIGAIL WALDRON

Kristen,
with love and
gratitude for your
friendship,

Abigail Waldron

RESOURCE *Publications* · Eugene, Oregon

FAR AS THE CURSE IS FOUND
Searching for God in Infertility, Miscarriage, and Stillbirth

Resource Publications
An Imprint of Wipf and Stock Publishers
199 W. 8th Ave., Suite 3
Eugene, OR 97401

www.wipfandstock.com

PAPERBACK ISBN: 978-1-4982-2104-7
HARDCOVER ISBN: 978-1-4982-2106-1

Manufactured in the U.S.A.   3/29/2016

For Avaleen

To the woman he said, "I will surely multiply your pain in childbearing; in pain you shall bring forth children."

—GEN 3:16A

He comes to make his blessings flow far as the curse is found.

—ISAAC WATTS, "JOY TO THE WORLD"

Contents

Introduction

My story is one many women could tell: a story of pain related to bearing children. For me, the pain first crept in during a year of infertility, and then, after abating with the birth of my first baby, engulfed me when I learned I'd miscarried my second. In those dark, early days and the challenging months that followed, in my ongoing struggle to reconcile the God I've known since my childhood with my disappointment and grief, I've often felt isolated, excluded from a Christian culture that celebrates children and motherhood but has remained oddly silent when confronted with people like me, people who desperately want babies but have struggled with infertility and loss.

I'm not the only one. Over the course of a year after my miscarriage, as I wrote my way through my sorrow, I talked to eleven other families who've suffered reproductive loss, families willing to share some of the most personal and difficult moments of their lives in hopes of strengthening their fellow sufferers. I sat with these families, in living rooms and restaurant booths, and—while still wading through my own hurt and questions about God—listened to them talk about babies waited for and babies lost. I listened to them wrestle with and seek answers to the same questions I'd been asking, the questions we often find ourselves confronted with when our plans fail and our dreams crumble: *Why would a good God allow such painful suffering? How can His presence be felt and trusted in the face of such great anguish?*

I thought that by putting these families' stories down on paper, by exploring the depths of our collective hurt, I'd discover answers to these questions, that I'd find some clarity. I imagined that talking to others would not only be an act of comradery but also an act of education, a way to help me gain new insight and perspective into why God permitted so much heartbreak to enter into my own story. I found something else instead: I've never been as alone as I thought.

As you read this collection of stories, I hope you'll feel surrounded and upheld in your own places of suffering, whether or not they mirror the specific experiences identified in these pages. I hope you'll find multiple points of intersection, a way to enter into the sort of community I longed for at my lowest and loneliest. Most of all, I hope you'll find glimpses of Him, the God who is mysteriously present in our deepest darkness, who is patient and gentle with the brokenhearted, and who receives as a beautiful expression of faith even the feeblest whisper of His name.

Part One

2009–2012

If I could be anything in the world, I would be a mother.

—Third grade journal (1988–1989)

Chapter 1

It's early Sunday morning, and CJ and I are driving out of DC. I'm in the passenger seat, watching the cars nearby on the familiar but unusually empty Beltway. My youngest brother Nate and his wife Ashley are in the backseat, telling us about their new hometown of Philadelphia. We are all newlyweds: Nate and Ashley married last May, followed by CJ and me in August.

The four of us have been awake for hours already. We struggled from bed before sunrise in hopes of beating the crowds and capturing the elusive beauty of Washington's cherry blossoms. Instead, we found every path to the Tidal Basin blocked by a morning race and swarms of cheering fans. We settled for distant glimpses of a few trees and the occasional scatter of delicate pink petals on the grey sidewalks.

But we hadn't minded much. Away from the race, on the wide gravel pathways of the vacant DC Mall, we walked and talked and soaked in the tranquility of a city still asleep. Last year at this time, we'd been bonding over wedding planning binders, but this visit is more relaxed. Since Nate and Ashley live nearly three hours away, CJ and I haven't seen them since Christmas, when we gathered at my parents' home along with our middle brother, Joel. I don't call either of my brothers regularly, but I cherish the times when I see them, times that are always characterized by laughter and deep conversation.

Now we're headed west, toward the Northern Virginia townhouse CJ and I bought last summer, months after we finished our respective grad school programs and weeks before our wedding. Our conversation turns to the future, to the idea of children.

"I think we might start trying once we've been married for a year," I announce, very aware that this milestone is only four months away.

"You'll definitely have a kid before us then," Nate says. "We are *so* not ready yet."

"Definitely not," Ashley adds, and laughter fills the car.

I'm surprised by my deep sense of relief. I know Nate's comment was casual, unplanned, but it feels more like a welcome promise. *Children are coming. You'll be a mother soon.*

———

It's a testament to my own mother that for as long as I can remember, I've wanted most of all to be a mom. Growing up, home felt like a warm blanket wrapped tight, and on some level, I must have always known that my mother made it this way, that in her bread baked from scratch and summer adventures and story-time snuggles, there was a safe, grounding love. When my brothers and I hurt ourselves, she would draw us close, kiss our wounds, and tell us, "There's medicine in Mommy's lips." And long after I knew that wasn't really true, I also knew it *was* true.

More than anything, I wanted to be this kind of mother to my own little brood. I had other goals—goals that motivated me to graduate from high school as valedictorian and from my university's honors program magna cum laude, but my desire for motherhood was my longest and most constant ambition. As I worked hard on my studies and experienced the resulting successes, I developed an expectation that my familial goals would be achieved with similar simplicity. I'd do what I'd watched my mother and many other women I knew from church do: get married shortly after college and have kids within a few years.

Instead, I found myself graduating without even a boyfriend. Unlike school, where if I followed directions and put forth effort, I was rewarded with the high marks I craved, romantic relationships didn't come as easily to me. I'd assumed that if I followed God and sought to live a good Christian life, I'd be rewarded with marriage and children. But it wasn't happening.

I spent my early and mid-twenties single, praying regularly for a husband and struggling as I watched friend after friend get married, including many of the younger girls I'd mentored in college. I loved my work as a middle-school English teacher and forged deep connections with many of my students, but I longed for the day I would have a family of my own.

Looking back, much of my pain seems almost laughable. I was so young, and I had so much going for me: a job I enjoyed, excellent friends, and a loving, supportive family. But for the first time, I was facing the reality that my life was not in my control, that I couldn't achieve what I wanted simply through hard work and good behavior. It was a reality I didn't like.

When CJ and I became engaged after a year of dating, I found my excitement tempered by nervousness. I've always been anxious about big decisions, and I worried about making a life-long commitment to one person, about whether or not we were truly right for one another. I worried that we were too different, that my emotional ups and downs would eventually wear on him, that the steadiness about him I loved would also make it difficult for us to connect deeply. But one thing I didn't worry about was starting a family together. I'd seen him with children of all ages, and I knew he'd be an amazing dad.

We were twenty-eight on our wedding day. I was well aware that by the time my mother was twenty-eight, she'd already birthed all three of her children. I felt behind before I'd even had a chance to begin.

———

It's Thanksgiving weekend, seven months after our cherry-blossom outing, and CJ and I plan to celebrate the holiday with my family at my parents' home in Lancaster, Pennsylvania.

I'm tired. I've just returned from a weekend at Duke University, where a few colleagues and I presented a conference paper about teaching business writing during a recession. The end of the semester is nearing, and the piles of papers I need to grade for my freshmen can be measured in inches. CJ and I have been living in chaos for the past few weeks while navigating the process of hardwood floor installation. This is all normal life stuff, and I know that soon enough the papers will be graded and the house will be back to normal. But there's something else too: I'm not pregnant yet, even though we've been trying for three months.

It shouldn't bother me. As CJ keeps reminding me, there's nothing to worry about. I've done my homework, of course: it takes the average couple six months to conceive, and doctors don't usually express concern about fertility issues until a full year has passed without a pregnancy. But I'm frustrated. I'm getting antsy.

Each month, I've allowed myself to anticipate the possibility of having a baby. Each month, with the start of my period, I've cried—deeply disappointed.

Despite my growing feelings of concern, I'm looking forward to celebrating the holiday with my family. Though my parents know we're trying, I don't plan to talk about my pregnancy-related fears on this trip. I want to enjoy being with people who love me, to put aside my worries for a few days of relaxation and homemade food.

Shortly after CJ and I arrive, we settle into the small living room of my parents' city row house: Mom and Dad, CJ and me, Nate and Ashley, and Joel and his girlfriend Jen. We're packed in snugly, nestled in couches and a few antique chairs, our chatter relaxed.

Joel and Jen are telling us about their campus ministry work at Penn State, and my dad makes sure CJ has packed everything he needs for their post-Thanksgiving hunting trip. There's a lull in conversation, and Nate's voice, suddenly serious, fills the silence. "Well, now that you're all here," he says, "we wanted to tell you guys something."

He pauses, and I hold my breath. I think I know what he is about to say, but I hope I'm wrong.

"Ashley's pregnant," he announces.

A physical weight presses against my chest. I glance up and see my mom looking in my direction, and I note the gentle concern meant for me before she brightens and turns to congratulate my brother and his wife.

There's momentary relief to know someone besides CJ understands that right now I am struggling. I offer my own congratulations to Nate and Ashley and register details about the due date and potential baby names, but I'm mostly thinking about what, at the time, feels like an injustice.

———

I've been dreading this day for months now, hoping that I'll be pregnant before it arrives, that my experience of this holiday will be joyful. But on Mother's Day, I don't feel like celebrating. It's been ten months, and there's still no baby.

I'm two months away from a clinical diagnosis of infertility, but I *feel* infertile, incapable of producing life. For weeks and weeks, I've been charting my waking temperature each morning, trying to pinpoint ovulation. I've cut caffeine from my diet after reading somewhere that excessive consumption can decrease fertility. And I've prayed and prayed and prayed.

I keep trying to figure out what God is up to, as if knowing His plan will somehow help me get what I want more quickly. *Is there some lesson I'm supposed to learn in this time of waiting?* I ask. *Is there something we're doing wrong? If I can just figure it out, then maybe God will bless me.* Or maybe, I think, *if I just stop wanting a baby so badly, if I stop trying so hard, we'll get pregnant.*

But deep down, I know it isn't really like that at all. If God waited to give babies until people had it all together, no one would ever have children. God hasn't chosen to give us a baby, and I cannot force Him to, no matter how hard I try or pray. I feel stuck, powerless.

In the Bible, women in my situation are referred to as barren, and these days, I think of that word often. It reminds me of "Thank You, M'am," a Langston Hughes short story I used to read with my eighth-grade students. In it, Hughes uses the word *barren* to describe a city stoop, and my own barrenness feels the way I've always pictured Hughes's stoop: dark, shadowy, cracked, and dirty—absent of flowers, absent of light, absent of beauty.

A few times a month, CJ and I attend small group meetings at the home of a fellow church member. I am the only childless woman in our particular group, and while I've done enough babysitting to engage in the discussions about cloth diapers and bedtime routines, I feel excluded. On Sunday mornings, I survey the congregation and see children everywhere, row after row of squirming, wiggling life. In our row, it's only CJ and me, no diaper bags, strollers, or babies to fill our arms and our laps. Some days I can barely stand it.

Even so, on Mother's Day, we go to church. We attend in part because it's habit, duty even, but also because no matter how much it hurts, I don't want to isolate myself from God or from my community. A broken heart, I figure, is better than a bitter one.

Most of the service proceeds like any other Sunday, but there's a brief moment during the announcements when mothers are honored. A pastor asks the mothers present to stand, and everyone claps enthusiastically. I clap too. I *am* grateful for my own mom and for the countless sacrifices she made for my brothers and me, and I'm grateful, too, for the many amazing mothers in this room, some of them my close friends, who love their children so very well.

But my eyes fill with tears as I think about how I remain separated from these women, that with each passing month, the odds of me ever joining their ranks seem to grow smaller.

In the car on the way to lunch after the service, I can't stop crying. CJ parks on the roof of the parking deck adjacent to the restaurant. We're alone up there, and I sob until I can find no more tears, littering the car floor with balled-up tissues.

"I don't understand," I tell CJ. "Why won't God give us a baby?"

"I don't know," he says, leaning over to put his arm around my shoulder.

"I hate it," I tell him. "I hate being barren. It's a terrible word." I tell him about the Langston Hughes story, about the way I picture that city stoop.

He listens, thoughtful. "But there's another word, Abby," he says, finally. "It's a good word. It's *God*."

In the bathroom on the morning I turn thirty, I see the telltale spots of red.

It's been twelve months now, twelve cycles of building anticipation and crushing disappointment. I've been praying that God would allow me to get pregnant before my thirtieth birthday, and while I can't say I've been filled with faith about His response, it feels like a particular insult to mark the beginning of a new decade with such a painful anniversary.

I guess I'll get in touch with a fertility specialist next week, I think with resignation.

I remind myself of the progress I've made the past few months. Through prayer and conversations with my mom and with friends, I've begun to sense God's presence in our infertility in a way I couldn't earlier in our journey. I've felt Him telling me that writing is part of my calling, that if I don't prioritize that now, before kids, I certainly won't have as much time or energy to do so when faced with the pressing demands of a young child at home. I've been reminded that God too is a writer, the ultimate storyteller, and that my story is woven into His greater one. I've been reminded that all the chaos and confusion and mess will eventually resolve. For the first time in a long time, I've begun to feel glimmers of hope and faith, and just a few weeks prior, I held my precious baby niece on the day of her birth and felt deep and genuine gladness.

"But," I tell my friend Becca a few hours later over a birthday lunch, "this is still really hard."

From across the table she nods, her brow furrowed. She's sat with me and my tears on multiple occasions throughout the past year, and she hasn't backed away. She knew about my prayer to be pregnant by thirty, and I know she understands the sting I'm feeling today.

Curiously, by mid-afternoon, my bleeding seems to have stopped. *Could I be?* I wonder.

But I don't allow myself to finish that thought. There have been too many false alarms.

On the way to dinner that night, I tell CJ I'm pretty sure my period has started, so I'm planning to have wine with dinner. He suggests I skip it, just in case. "Come on," I pout. "It's my thirtieth birthday, and I'm sure I'm not really pregnant."

But I do pass on the wine. When there's no more blood by the next morning, I feel a growing sense of hope. The day after that, a bright summer Saturday, I wake up and pull a pregnancy test out of my bathroom cabinet. I've taken enough by now to know almost immediately that this one is different, to see that instead of a straight blue line, a little pink plus sign is beginning to form.

———

Nine months later, minutes before midnight, I'm reclined in a hospital bed with my newborn daughter snuggled in my arms. I'm sweaty and disheveled, exhausted from fourteen hours of labor, still jittery from the cocktail of medications pumped into me before my C-section. I look terrible, but I don't care. My baby girl is finally here, and she is beautiful.

CJ's smile is wide, and he can't stop crying. We are so completely happy.

We name her Elliana Grace, which means *God has answered*, and I feel that truth deeply, in the center of my being. After all of the tears and the waiting and the uncertainty, God has shown up and heard our cries, not because we figured out everything or stopped wanting a baby so desperately, but because He is good, because there really is such a thing as amazing, breathtaking grace.

There's no denying it now, Ellie Girl. You're more toddler than baby. You totter your way across the room without falling, without needing support. You're beginning to understand language, whispering a raspy "hiiyyyy" when you see yourself in a mirror, repeating a decisive "puh" after me when I ask you to say please instead of fussing to get what you want.

Lately, you've taken an interest in reading books, handing them to me one after the other, sometimes the same one again and again, listening as you stand beside me, motionless. Sometimes, you're even still long enough to actually snuggle into my lap, your warm body relaxing against mine. But mostly, you move. You walk. Push chairs across the hardwood floors. Bang and shake things. You love anything that makes noise.

And oh, Ellie Girl, we love you so much. We love you and also we miss our uninterrupted sleep. We miss our long, quiet, productive Saturdays. We miss being able to sit through sermons on Sundays and make plans without lining up a babysitter. But the gift of you is a greater and richer joy than any of these things. You delight us.

—Letter to Ellie, March 8, 2012

Chapter 2

"I think we should start trying again," CJ says one night while we're getting ready for bed.

I'm on my way to the bathroom, but I stop and turn to look at him. Ellie is only ten months old, and I'm just coming out of the fog of nursing and spit-up and baby naps that never last more than forty minutes.

"It took so long the last time," he reasons.

I nod. We know we want another child, probably a few more, actually, and I'm nearing thirty-two. We don't know why it took us a year to get pregnant, so there's no reason to expect it will be any faster this time.

"Let's do it," I say.

We agree to take it slowly—to not worry about charting and timing things perfectly, to see what happens.

And this time, just like that, a few weeks before Ellie's first birthday I learn I'm pregnant again.

I'm elated. I know that caring for two children so close in age will be challenging, and I dread the return of the terrible, crippling nausea I suffered for the first four months of my pregnancy with Ellie. But mostly, I feel relief. *Ellie isn't going to be our only miracle.*

In the past few years, I've thought often about those women who have the ability to schedule pregnancies like playdates, penciling them in to avoid being large and swollen in the heat of summer or having to give birth in the darkest, dreariest days of winter. *Maybe now*, I decide, *I'm one of them.* We didn't exactly schedule this pregnancy, but it happened easily and naturally. No anxiety. No complications.

This is how it should be, I think, happy to put the difficulty of infertility behind me. *I can finally just have babies.*

My sister-in-law notices first. "Wait, what does her shirt say?"

It's Saturday afternoon, the day before Easter, and CJ and I are sprawled out on couches in my parents' living room. In the background, golf is on the TV. We've been catching up and relaxing with my parents, my brother Joel, and Jen—now his wife.

After Jen asks, everyone adjusts to look at the grey T-shirt CJ and I changed Ellie into after her nap, our announcement spelled out in sparkly fluorescent letters: *Big Sister.*

"Are you serious?" my dad asks.

"When are you due?" my mom wants to know.

There are hugs and joyful congratulations. We Skype with Nate and Ashley and share the news with them too. The attention make me uncomfortable, just as it will when we repeat the scene with CJ's family tomorrow, but telling everyone also makes this baby seem more real, more exciting.

Later, on our way out to the backyard for Ellie's first Easter egg hunt, my brother asks if we think we'll have more kids after this one. "I don't know," I say. "It depends. But we think we'd like to have three or four."

"Then you're halfway there," he responds, matter-of-fact.

"I guess." I say. I know he means his words to be encouraging, but they make me uneasy.

At the time, I credit this feeling to only being in my seventh week of pregnancy, the nausea and fatigue and aches and pains I know are coming having only just begun. Later, though, I'll think back to this moment and realize I understood, even then, that the life inside me was fragile and tenuous, anything but certain.

By eight weeks, I am feeling as terrible as I expected.

Every morning, CJ brings me breakfast in bed, usually eggs and toast. I've found that if I eat before I get out of bed, I'm more likely to keep my breakfast down—if only slightly. After he leaves for work, I count the minutes until Ellie's first nap, when I can crawl back into bed and sleep.

Every afternoon, I muster the energy to slide off the couch and onto the floor to play with my daughter. I try to feed her lunch without throwing up my own, which means hummus, one of her favorites, is out. Then I count the minutes until her second nap, when I can get back into bed again.

In the evenings, I count the minutes until CJ returns home from work. Sometimes I manage to put dinner on the table, but more often, merely the act of opening the pantry door sends me running to the toilet. We eat a lot of takeout.

Night after night, week after endless week, I return to bed while CJ feeds Ellie and tucks her into her crib. Sometimes I only lay there, willing my dinner to stay in my body. Sometimes I'm able to sleep. Sometimes I watch the most intelligent programming I can muster, *16 and Pregnant*. I'm too sick to read anything longer than a Facebook status.

I hate it. "I will never do this again," I tell CJ regularly.

"It'll be worth it," he promises.

And he's right. I felt this sick with Ellie, and she's definitely worth it. When I get to meet this new baby, these terrible early days will seem a small price to pay for the magic of another fresh life.

But I'm miserable. Reduced to survival, I don't spend much time dreaming about holding the baby inside of me. Instead, my focus is shorter, on reaching the middle of my second trimester—on finally feeling better.

———

On Wednesday, May 30, I'm fifteen weeks pregnant and finally less nauseous. The day is clear and warm, so Ellie and I meet friends at the pool. It feels good to be outside and doing something social after so many lonely weeks at home.

I follow Ellie around the baby pool, ready to catch her each time her unsteady legs give way. She stops to fill her buckets, and I look up, taking note of who else is here today. A few of the other moms are visibly pregnant.

Is it obvious yet? I wonder, looking down at the slight bulge around my middle. *I guess I'll need a maternity suit soon.*

I'm glad the first trimester is behind me, that I can handle the smell of coffee again, that the thought of cooking dinner doesn't make me want to hurl. *This will be a fun summer*, I think, imagining myself waddling to the pool with Ellie and thinking of the other adventures we'll share together before the baby's November arrival: berry picking, camping, the beach.

That afternoon, CJ stays home with Ellie while I go to a routine OB appointment. I sit in the waiting room, flipping the pages of a magazine as I eavesdrop on two women, both pregnant with twins, catching snippets of their conversation about groups for mothers of multiples and baby equipment for two.

A nurse calls me back. "How are you feeling?" she asks, sliding the blood pressure cuff around my arm.

"A little better," I say. "Finally."

When my doctor enters the room, she hugs me warmly, as she has at every appointment throughout both of my pregnancies. "I love your shirt," she says.

"Thanks," I say. I like it too—white and flowing, it's perfect for camouflaging the bulge that isn't yet a bump.

I lay back on the table, uncovering my stomach, and my doctor presses the Doppler wand against my skin and slides it back and forth. Seconds pass. There is only static.

CJ and I have heard this baby's heartbeat on three occasions before today. Even though I know it can take time to locate during the early months of pregnancy, I hold my breath.

"Let's go to the room with the ultrasound machine," my doctor suggests calmly, stepping toward the door.

I'm aware of what she has not said, that there's a good chance we won't find a heartbeat there either, but when I answer with, "Okay," I'm careful to mirror the calm of her voice in my own.

In the ultrasound room, the doctor rubs gel on my belly and floats the wand across it. My heart pounds, and I'm shaking. Immediately I see my baby, the perfect little head and body, curled peacefully.

What I do not see is the steady flicker of a beating heart.

"Abby," my doctor says, her words slow and quiet, "I can't find a heartbeat."

"I know."

My body does not register surprise. In recent weeks, I thought I felt the baby stir on several occasions, but over the last few days, I've noticed that the almost imperceptible movements have stopped. I silenced the anxious thoughts that followed: *You always think the worst,* and, *It's unusual to feel movement this early anyway. There's nothing to worry about.* But now, seeing the form of my lifeless child on the screen in front of me, I think part of me must have known what was coming.

"I'm so sorry," my doctor says.

I nod. My heart is still pounding, and my baby's heart is still motionless, and I cannot think of anything to say.

But my doctor knows what to do with my silence. She tells me about her own miscarriage, an early loss after her first baby. Her wisdom: It might be months before I feel better. The ache will never really go away.

Later, I'll turn her words over and over again, appreciative of her fierce compassion and tender care. But here in the exam room, I'm trying to wrap my brain around what's happening. *My baby is dead*, I think. *The life that's been growing inside me is gone forever.*

The ultrasound measurements indicate the baby probably died sometime in the last few days. "It's unusual to have a loss this late," my doctor keeps saying. She orders blood tests and hands me tissues and asks me whether I want to miscarry naturally or have a dilation and extraction (D&E) procedure at the hospital.

Then she steps out, and I sit alone, waiting for a lab tech to draw blood. The words of Job, Scripture's most famous sufferer, rise in my mind: *The Lord gave, and the Lord has taken away* (Job 1:21b). In the days to come, I'll wrestle with the implication, with the thought that God is somehow behind my child's death, but in this moment, as my tears begin to flow, I find the verse comforting. *Even here,* I think, *God is.*

The lab tech enters the room, hands full of vials. She surveys my tear-streaked face and notes the tissues balled up in my fists. "Don't be sad," she says. "It will be okay."

It will not be okay, I think, annoyed at her forced cheerfulness and insensitivity. *My baby is dead. I may never be okay again.* I stare at her but say nothing.

She takes my blood, and then a nurse ushers me gently out a back door. I'm relieved to avoid facing a waiting room crowded with pregnant women, but I also feel ashamed, like the dead baby inside me is a terrible secret I must carry alone.

I drive home sobbing, the highway barely visible through my tears. I consider calling CJ, but I don't want to tell him over the phone.

When I open the front door, he's right there, holding Ellie. They've just gotten back from a walk. "What's wrong?" he asks, and I fall into his arms.

"Our baby's gone."

———

The next morning, I drop off Ellie at my friend Becca's house so CJ and I can drive to the hospital for an ultrasound. "Just to be sure," my doctor explained.

Ellie loves Becca and her son Caleb, but today, she doesn't want me to go. She wraps her pudgy arms around my neck and holds on tightly. My eyes brim with tears, and a few steps away, Becca cries too. "I'm really sorry," I say to Ellie. "Mommy doesn't want to go. I wish more than anything I didn't have to do this."

I leave her still crying, and I can't stop my own tears either. *I will never get to hold my second child.*

The ultrasound confirms what we already know: our baby is dead and has been for at least a few days. We schedule a D&E for the next morning. No one tells me exactly what this procedure entails. No one explains that, as with a dilation and curettage (D&C), my cervix will be dilated, but that instead of scraping my uterus clean, my child will be suctioned out with a vacuum aspirator. I do not ask for the details, but I know enough. I know that somehow my precious child will be removed from my body in tiny, lifeless pieces. I briefly consider trying to miscarry at home on my own, but my doctor says this will probably take weeks. Already, I'm burdened by the terrible weight of carrying death inside me.

Later, I'll learn of other options, and I'll wish I'd been induced, allowed to deliver and hold and bury my child, but no one mentions this possibility, and neither CJ nor I think to ask for it. We've spent the past few months planning for our child's life. Not once did we consider how we'd handle the very real possibility of its death.

The next morning, a Friday, CJ and I are back at the hospital. We sit in my gold Saturn sedan in a quiet corner of the parking garage, our hands on my stomach, talking to our baby exactly as we have lay in bed and done for many nights over these last three months.

"Goodbye, little one," CJ says, his voice wavering. "I'm sorry I'll never get to hold you and play with you."

"Goodbye, baby," I say through my tears. "I love you so much. I miss you. I'm sorry."

We cry together, and then CJ takes my hand as we walk through the doors of the same hospital we entered nearly fourteen months ago on the day of Ellie's birth.

We sit for what seems like hours in a waiting room with other women scheduled for gynecological surgery. I search their faces for clues about their stories. *Are they just here for routine procedures? Am I the only one with a dead baby inside me?*

Finally, my name is called. I change into a hospital gown, and nurses start an IV and prep me for surgery. Moments before I'm wheeled away, CJ snaps a picture of me with his phone. In it, my eyes are puffy, and my hands cradle my stomach. It's odd that he captures such a terrible moment, but I'm grateful for it in the days that come after: an image of the last seconds I had with my child.

When we leave the hospital a few hours later, my body feels strangely normal. My appetite and energy have returned, and except for minor bleeding, I'm not experiencing any pain or discomfort.

But everything about life feels wrong. I'm not pregnant anymore. I'm leaving the hospital without my child. The only part of our baby that remains is a set of tiny footprints my doctor somehow managed to take for us, smaller than a dime.

All day Saturday, we find deliveries on our doorstep: flowers, notes, homemade scones, bread from a local bakery. Our small group from church brings meals. I spend most of the day in our living room, surrounded by bouquets and cards, and I feel bolstered, upheld in my sadness. Each gesture affirms our baby's life matters, that even though our child's life was short, my devastating grief is real and valid.

By Sunday, I'm tired of sitting at home but not yet ready to return to church. We go instead to the mall. But it's bright and busy here, and the bustle of the well-dressed crowd is an insult. *Don't they know my baby's dead?* I want to scream. *Don't they know that none of this matters?*

While CJ entertains Ellie, I try on capri pants at Ann Taylor. I don't really feel like shopping, but now that I won't be wearing maternity clothes, I find myself in need of additions to my summer wardrobe. I grab a pair in my pre-pregnancy size and slip them on in the changing room. They're snug on my hips, and I can't button them. I shouldn't be surprised given that two days ago I was pregnant, but standing there in front of the mirror, it's too much to bear. I leave the mall crying hot, angry tears.

"None of this is right," I tell CJ. "It's not supposed to be like this."

The next day, my mom arrives to help with Ellie when CJ returns to work. We go to the pool, and since I'm not allowed to swim for two weeks following my D&E, my mom splashes with her granddaughter while I watch from a chair, smiling at the love between them. In the evenings, after Ellie is in bed, the three of us sink into couches and soft chairs, and my mom asks thoughtful questions, listening to CJ and I share what we're feeling. I've known since I was young that my mother had an early miscarriage before I was born, but she doesn't say much about her own experience—she keeps the lens on us. She's simply there, and for a few days, everything feels a bit better.

After she leaves, a week post-surgery, CJ takes a day off of work and we drive with Ellie to the ocean—to be together and to get away. It's the first time Ellie's been to the beach since she could walk, and CJ and I laugh as she runs straight into the surf, fearless. We eat French fries and soak in the sunshine and listen to the healing rhythm of the waves and remind ourselves that even in our grief, life can still be good, that God still gives joy. I'm more thankful than ever for Ellie's life, for her brightness in these dark days. *God has answered,* I remember.

There is a void, and I fill it. I hunger for beauty and creative pursuits. New recipes. Flower gardens. Plans for parties I will someday host. I bake bread for a neighbor and brew homemade mint tea for a friend and experiment with blending spinach and strawberries into smoothies for Ellie.

I can't ever replace the life I lost, but I can honor the empty space my baby left behind. *Your short life has changed me, baby,* I type into the journal I now keep on my iPad and fill during the few snatches of time I find to be alone. *I want you to know that the space you created in my heart is not being wasted.*

But as the days turn into weeks and life continues, as the flowers die and the stream of cards slows to a trickle, as the diaper changing and dinner making and errand running fail to relent, I'm increasingly empty. The depth is surprising. *I was terribly sick,* I think, trying to understand my sadness. *I didn't even have time to think much about this baby. How is it possible to miss someone you don't even know?*

But I do, with an intensity I can't explain—a literal, physical ache. It's there every time I go out in public and enter a world overflowing with pregnant women. It's there every time I see mothers of two small children in

Target. It's there at church especially, where a new baby seems to be born to a member of our congregation every week. The rest of the world keeps spinning happily along, but I'm alone and stuck. I don't have any close friends who've experienced a miscarriage, especially so late, and I've yet to talk to anyone who's lost a baby after their first trimester. I long for someone who can understand, who can tell me it will be okay, that there's another side I will one day come out on, that I won't lose my faith in this darkness.

———

Less than three weeks after the silence of the Doppler machine, we're back once again in the doctor's office. "I am sorry to tell you this," my doctor tells us, "but every test result is normal. There were no genetic abnormalities."

She pauses. "I hate that I can't give you any answers."

I don't understand the implications of this news, not yet. In fact, on this day, I feel relieved. *Everything was normal,* I think. *Our baby was healthy. I'm healthy. There's no indication my body will do this again.* It will take time before I realize what she meant, about the burden of unexplained miscarriage, its fearful uncertainty.

"Do you want me to tell you your baby's gender?" she asks.

We nod. From the beginning, both CJ and I have wanted to find out if we could.

"A girl," she says, her eyes meeting mine.

"We thought so," I tell her. Throughout my pregnancy, CJ and I often caught ourselves referring to the baby as *she,* but we thought that because our first child was a girl, perhaps it felt natural to gravitate toward this familiar pronoun. But our instincts had been right.

Another girl. I imagine a newborn with a full head of dark hair like Ellie's. *A perfectly healthy baby girl.* I'd always wanted a little sister myself, and I can't stop thinking about how Ellie would have had one, a constant playmate, a companion for life. I'm glad to learn of my second daughter, to receive this one piece of information about the child I'll never meet, but knowing more also intensifies my ache for what is gone. I want to crawl outside of myself. Anything to escape the weight.

———

A month of life passes, a month without her. Ellie wakes early from her nap one afternoon, and I sit in the glider in her bedroom and rock her. She nestles against my neck, warm, and I hear her breath—in and out—and inhale the sunscreen scent of her sleep-damp hair.

My chest tightens—not anxiety, but a manifestation of emotion overflowing, of feeling something so deeply I can hardly breathe. The love I feel for Ellie is rich, sacred, but it also amplifies my sense that something's missing. I think of my second daughter and how I'll never get to hold her like this. Every happy moment with Ellie is now mingled with sadness, my delight deeper because I know how easily it can be taken away, my pain intensified because I'm reminded of what is gone.

It's impossible to believe I'll ever truly be happy again, that my grief won't always color even my brightest joy.

———

It takes a few months, but CJ and I finally decide on a name: Avaleen, *longed for child*. Her middle name is Hope.

Avaleen Hope. Her first name describes my present reality, my yearning. I pray her middle name describes a future I can't yet feel or see.

On our last night at the beach, I walked with CJ across the sand because I was too tired and sad to even go for a margarita like we'd initially planned. So we walked. And then we sat, side by side in the sand, and we cried. Both of us. We tried to talk, to process our feelings, but I couldn't even manage that. I was just sad. I cried so hard snot was dripping out of my nose, and I had no tissues. I used my hand and then flung it into the sand. CJ let me wipe some on his undershirt, and we had to laugh in spite of ourselves. Grief is ugly.

On the way home from getting groceries a few days later, I sobbed alone in the car, wailing with the full force of my voice. I just felt incredibly sad, and nothing I could do would make it stop.

—Journal entry, August 7, 2012

Chapter 3

In late August, I return to the beach for the weekend with two girlfriends. It rains the entire time, relentless, pouring from the sky with such force I can barely see the road ahead of us on the drive to dinner. Later, the thunder and lightning are so intense that we each creep out of our bedrooms in the early morning hours, shaken.

But for a brief moment before we leave on Sunday, the three of us sit on the beach anyway, the rain steadier now, gentler. The sun is hidden behind a wall of dark clouds, and the waves are choppy, ominous. I stare past them to the calmer expanses of sea, pensive.

My friends are reading, and I'm thinking, as I've thought almost every day this summer, about how desperately I want to get pregnant again. Avaleen is irreplaceable, and I will always miss her. Still, as I've told my friends at multiple points throughout our trip, having another child might heal some of the pain, might fill in some of the gaps she's left behind. They agree. Another baby would help mend my heart.

My obstetrician has cleared us to start trying again, and in many ways, I feel ready. But I'm scared too. *What if we can't get pregnant again? Or worse, what if we lose another baby?* We don't know why Avaleen died, and no one can tell me exactly how likely it is that I'll miscarry again.

There's no such thing as a guarantee, but I'm determined to minimize risk in every way possible. CJ and I have been seeing a naturopath to help us clear up any underlying health concerns, and I've been reading a book about miscarriage, making a list of questions for my doctor about a few possible causes I haven't yet been tested for. I won't leave any stone unturned.

But deep down, even as I feel freedom from God to pursue these kinds of answers, I know the real question is not what caused Avaleen to die, but rather whether or not I will trust God with my future. *Will I be okay if we never have any other living children?* I ask myself. *Or what if another baby dies? Will God be good even then?*

I do not want to let go of my plans for more children. I do not want God to answer my prayers with *no*. But sitting on the beach that day, grey skies above and crashing surf ahead, I hear the whisper of His voice. *Abby, you and CJ must work on being the kind of family I have called you to be. Let me worry about if and when other children will come.*

I know immediately that these words are true, that I have to release my desires to God, but in the days that follow, I struggle. I ask God to forgive me for my demands, to help me loosen my grip on my plans. And, like a child, I keep begging. *Please Lord. Give us another baby.*

———

In early October, CJ and I wait in the Long Island office of a world-renowned reproductive immunologist who specializes in infertility and recurrent pregnancy loss. A friend of a friend who experienced multiple miscarriages referred us.

This specialist believes that unexplained pregnancy loss is often caused by immunologic factors, and while I'm not certain Avaleen's death can be explained by problems with my immune system, I figure it's worth exploring. My obstetrician doesn't think we need to see a specialist, but she understands why we want to. Since all the standard tests she ordered came back normal, CJ and I hope more testing might uncover a cause for our late miscarriage, one that everyone keeps telling us is highly unusual. We both believe God is ultimately sovereign over the lives of any future children, but we also feel strongly that we should take every opportunity provided to us to help protect those children.

In the waiting room, I turn the pages of a magazine, but I can't focus on any of the articles. *What will we learn today?* I wonder. *What if I have a major health problem?* But then I reason, *If something is wrong with me, I want to know. Then maybe we can do something about it.*

A nurse ushers us back to a small office, the walls covered with an impressive array of framed licenses and certificates. The doctor listens to our story carefully, takes notes, and then leads us to an examination room where he performs a special ultrasound that detects blood flow in various parts of the uterus. "You may have polycystic ovary syndrome," he says. "Women who don't present with the classic symptoms often go undiagnosed."

I nod, trying to take in this information and think of what questions to ask next.

"We'll order a bunch of tests on both you and your husband," the doctor offers, his voice brisk and confident. "We can help you have another baby."

We leave with eight pages of scripts for fifty or more blood tests. I recognize the names of some of them, tests for blood-sugar levels and food allergies and clotting disorders. I wonder how long it will take for the results to come back and for any necessary treatment to be completed. I'm anxious to start trying again soon.

———

CJ and I show up at our local laboratory a few days later for the tests. The technician takes one look at our pile of scripts and huffs. "They should never send you with all these different sheets," she says. "I hope you have at least an hour."

My body tenses. *It is a lot of tests,* I think, *but isn't this your job? I'm only giving you what my doctor gave me.* "Okay," I say, before returning to the waiting room on the verge of tears. CJ is outside with Ellie, who's fallen asleep in her car seat. I just want these tests to be done so we can move on.

Two hours later, the technician is finally ready to draw blood for fewer than half of the tests. She hands me pages filled with her questions about the others. She can't figure out what many of them are, and several others aren't even offered by this lab. I take one look at all of her scribbled notes and sigh, wondering how many hours I'll need to spend on the phone in search of answers.

"What's all this for anyway?" the technician asks, gruff.

"I had an unexplained late miscarriage," I tell her. "So we're seeing a specialist."

I expect a nod, some kind of curt or cursory acknowledgement, but instead her own story comes spilling out. She had two children, she tells me, then five miscarriages, then got pregnant with twins, one of whom she lost. Her miscarriages ruined her marriage.

She fills vial after vial with my blood as we talk about her children and her grandchildren. My irritation fades, and I'm aware of God's presence. I can't quite put my finger on what He's doing, but I know this: for a few sacred moments in a suburban office park laboratory, my own story of loss opens up another woman's story, and in spite of my broken plans, I feel grateful to sit with her and hear it.

Most days, though, I can't see God in Avaleen's death. It was one thing to trust Him in infertility, in the absence of a desire fulfilled. It's quite another to trust him in miscarriage, in a desire fulfilled and then taken away, literally torn from the deepest part of my being. When we couldn't get pregnant, I saw glimpses of why God may have asked us to wait: my own sense of calling as a writer became clearer, my gratitude for Ellie became deeper. But I can't think of any way that losing Avaleen could ever be considered good. I believe good can and has come through her death, but I'm certain an all-powerful God could have produced the same good in a kinder, less difficult way.

I consider the possibility that suffering like mine is not the result of God's sovereign plan, as I've always been taught and believed, but rather an unfortunate consequence of existing in a fallen world, something God is somehow powerless to stop. After all, the original curse of Adam in Gen 3:17 includes language suggesting that much of life's difficulty is caused by human choice: *Because you have listened to the voice of your wife and have eaten of the tree of which I commanded you, "You shall not eat of it," cursed is the ground because of you; in pain you shall eat of it all the days of your life.* And the New Testament shows us a compassionate God in human form, a God who is moved so deeply by human suffering that He weeps over the death of a man he knows He will restore to life just moments later.[1] Clearly, God takes no pleasure in the pain of His people.

But I can't escape the verses that present God as a sovereign, powerful being orchestrating every event in history for His purposes. Isa 45:7 is perhaps most definitive on this point. *I form light and create darkness,* God says. *I make well-being and create calamity, I am the Lord, who does all these things.* Whether God directly causes suffering or rather permits it to happen is less evident to me, but I keep coming back to verses indicating that in some way, it is part of His plan.[2]

But where was this good and powerful God at the moment Avaleen's heart stopped beating? Why didn't He intervene and save her life? I can't find

1. John 11:35.
2. Deut 32:39, Eccl 7:14, Lam 3:37–38.

a way to imagine a kind, loving, and gracious God standing by and watching a tiny, defenseless baby die—or even worse, willing it.

I wrestle intensely with these questions, thinking my way through them until my brain is tired or crying out to God until my eyes are puffy and there are no tears left. On the days when I'm not so worried about the questions, I feel sad and alone.

I make more of an effort to fill my time. Our church has just started a group for moms of young children—an opportunity to get out of the house and interact with other women in a similar stage of life. But when I'm there, I spend most of the time feeling like I don't belong. I'm one of the few mothers with only one child, and the talk generally revolves around the intensity and chaos of caring for a busy family.

But I don't feel busy. There's space in our home and in our lives. Too much space. *Don't you get it?* I want to scream when I hear moms talk about how hard their lives are, how exhausting it is to care for multiple children. *Don't you know how much I'd give to be getting up in the middle of the night with a newborn? Don't you know how badly I want sibling squabbles and more diapers to change?*

Of course they don't mean to hurt me, and it truly *is* difficult to be in their position. My loss doesn't invalidate their very real exhaustion, and I'm certain I'd be saying the exact same things if I were currently caring for a newborn and a toddler. But in these moments, too, it's difficult not to feel excluded.

———

I'm sitting in Becca's living room one night, my feet tucked up underneath me on her couch. I'm telling her about the journal I've been keeping, about the desire that's been building inside me to share Avaleen's story with a more public audience.

I've kept a blog for years, the sort of thing that family and friends read, but I haven't posted anything about my miscarriage there or on social media. CJ and I never announced our pregnancy to anyone outside of close family and friends, so we hadn't been forced to talk about Avaleen's death on those forums either. And for a long time, I didn't want to. It felt too painful and too personal to process with anyone except a handful of people. Part of me also wanted to separate the miscarriage from my public persona, to avoid being known to others as a grieving mother. But lately, my thoughts on that have been changing. Avaleen is part of my story, and if I don't talk about her, I can't write honestly about much of anything.

I'm trying to explain this to Becca, to put into words the burden I feel to share my story. I'm mid-sentence when I stop suddenly, catching myself. The phrase *this gift* is about to slide off my tongue.

Where'd that come from? I wonder. *Do I really mean to say that? How could the death of my baby girl be a gift?*

I don't know. But I turn to Becca and let the words come out: "This gift."

I can't explain it, but I know she is a gift, my Avaleen. And I'm more certain than ever that I want everyone to know about her.

———————

It is early November when the specialist finally calls with our results. There's no clear answer, he tells us. I do have a dairy allergy, borderline high blood-sugar levels, and a genetic mutation that increases my risk of miscarriage.

"Do you think any of these issues caused the miscarriage?" I ask.

"They could have," he says. "But we can't be certain." He wants to put me on high-powered antibiotics and blood thinners before we start trying again, just to be safe.

The treatment will be expensive, so CJ and I take some time to think about it. We've waited so long to try for another baby, we figure. A few more weeks won't hurt.

———————

The week of Thanksgiving, the week our Avaleen should have been born, I'm finally ready to tell her story. I write a post for my blog. *I have two daughters,* I begin. *One of them, Elliana Grace, is a busy, chatty toddler whose antics have made up more than half the contents of this blog since she was born nineteen months ago. The other, Avaleen Hope, was supposed to be born this week, but we lost her in late May, at around fourteen and a half weeks gestation.*

I write about why I've kept quiet for these past months, about my need for privacy and my fears of how others would react, about how I didn't want to be labeled as a woman who's miscarried. I write about Avaleen and how I miss her and how she's changed me.

And I end where I began: *I have two daughters. I hear one of them breathing softly over the baby monitor while I write. I feel the absence of the other in my flat stomach, my empty arms, in the fact that I am able to travel for Thanksgiving this week. I wish this post was Avaleen's birth announcement, that I was telling you how much she weighed, how her delivery went. Instead, I simply want to tell you that she lived.*

————

As 2012 draws to a close, I feel the weight of an uncertain future. After much conversation and prayer, CJ and I decide we won't pursue treatment with the reproductive immunologist. There is no guarantee the drugs will help, and they come with clear risks, risks neither we nor my obstetrician feel comfortable taking on. We opt instead for a simpler plan: no dairy in my diet, the supplements from our naturopath, and a daily regimen of low-dose aspirin.

I worry we're making the wrong decision, that we'll end up miscarrying another baby. And I'm scared that we'll wrestle with infertility once again. We don't—can't—know what will happen next. I hate that.

In the midst of all the uncertainty, though, I'm increasingly certain of two things: I want another baby, and I want to write a book.

I want to tell my story, Avaleen's story, but I also want to tell the story of others who've known similar heartache. I want to feel less alone on this journey, to write a book that will someday help others in this situation feel less alone too. I want to talk with families who birthed children after years of infertility and families who never had biological children, families who adopted and families whose adoptions failed, families who pursued various reproductive treatments and families who decided against them. I want to talk to families from different backgrounds, young families and established ones, families big and small. I want to see how God has met others in their pain, and in the process, I hope that He will meet me in mine.

Part Two

2013

Oh how desperately I want to know, to figure it out. Somehow it seems to me that if I knew why we had to lose our baby, if God would just tell me, I'd be able to trust Him better, more willing to submit to His plan.

I've spent more time than I care to admit speculating. Maybe God allowed this to happen because He wanted me to write about it and minister to others in a way I wouldn't be able to otherwise. Maybe I will know God in a way I couldn't have before.

Maybe one or both of those statements are true. Maybe. But the truth is that, even if they are, it's not enough. It's not enough to make our loss okay, to justify the absence of our little baby girl. It's not enough to make me stop hurting.

—Blog post, January 29, 2013

Chapter 4

JANUARY: MARK AND LESLEY

Ellie and I are making our way through the crowded lobby after her weekly Gymboree class when she catches sight of a classmate's infant brother. Her teacher notices my daughter's animated pointing and the way she's talking about the "tiny baby" and turns to me. "I think she's trying to give you a hint," she says, smiling.

I feel the tears rise and rush for the door, my head down. *If you only knew.*

Ellie loves babies. She has five of them currently: Tiny Baby, Blue Baby, Yellow Baby, Green Baby, and a baby with a rattle inside, still unnamed. She totes them with her around the house, to the playground, and on errands, feeds them and wraps them to make them "toasty," and sleeps surrounded by them in her crib at night. She would happily spend at least half an hour looking at her own baby pictures, proclaiming with pride on page after page, "Baby Eh-ee." Whenever we see a baby in public, she demands to say hello.

I hate that losing Avaleen has robbed Ellie of the opportunity to be a big sister. I continue to hope she'll get that chance, but I know that if and when she does, it will be different. She'll be older, the gap larger. She won't ever have a constant companion quite as close in age as Avaleen would have been.

We haven't told Ellie about Avaleen yet, but she and I pray for a baby almost every day. The prayers are simple, small. Ellie doesn't speak in sentences yet, so the words are mine: "Dear Jesus, we ask that you would bring us a baby very soon. Amen."

While I pray, my daughter is quiet. When I finish, often she'll tap her fingertips together, the sign for "more." And so we pray again. Before her nap or at bedtime, I shift the focus of our prayers to other things as well, thanking Jesus for fun parts of our day, asking for a good night's sleep, praying that Ellie will continue to know she is loved, that she'll grow to love Jesus. When I finish, she signs again, "More."

"What would you like to pray for, sweetheart?"

"Baby," she says.

"You want Mommy to pray for a baby?"

"Yeah."

And so I do. Most days, we recite this prayer multiple times.

On one level, this delights me. I love that my little girl wants to pray, that she's getting a chance to see how we bring our desires to Jesus and wait to see what He will do. I love that Ellie is a daily reminder of how to come to Jesus like a child, full of faith, sharing what's on her heart without growing weary of the asking.

But I worry too. *What if God doesn't answer?* I wonder. *What if there is no baby? Am I setting up my eighteen month old for a crisis of faith?*

But because my heart also longs for a baby, because I can't stop thinking about babies either, I ask—and wait—along with her. I try to trust that God will somehow meet us both.

———

I conduct my first interview close to home, with my senior pastor, Mark Mullery, and his wife Lesley. I don't know either Mark or Lesley personally, but I've always liked them. Mark is small in stature, intelligent and bookish, but when he preaches, his voice rising to a crescendo at a sermon's climax, the force of his words fills the sanctuary. Lesley seems sweet and gentle, someone who prefers to focus the spotlight on others and is visibly uncomfortable when asked to speak publicly. Unlike many people in church leadership, she and Mark both tend to fade into the background—a good thing, I think. In a power-hungry city where people worship image and prestige, it's refreshing to see leaders oriented toward quiet service.

Far as the Curse Is Found

Days after Avaleen died, we received an email from Mark:

I am so sorry to hear of this loss. May the Good Shepherd comfort you today and may the hope of seeing your child in heaven bring some sweetness to your souls.

A few days later, Lesley wrote as well:

I just heard about your baby this morning and wanted to let you know that I will be praying for you during this sad and challenging time. May the Lord surround you with his comfort, peace, and encouragement.

In their initial messages, neither mentioned that they too had experienced the tragic death of a baby almost thirty years ago—the stillbirth at thirty-two weeks of their first child, a daughter they named Sarah. Even though we attended the same church for almost eight years, even though I listened to Mark preach Sunday after Sunday, I didn't know this part of their story. I discovered it only after I replied to their emails, thanking them for their thoughts and prayers, and struck up a brief correspondence with Lesley in which she shared some of their own journey.

It meant so much to learn I wasn't alone, that another family had survived the devastation I felt, their faith intact. I wanted to know more, to sit down with the Mullerys and hear the details of their story. I asked if they'd meet with me, and happily, they agreed.

I've never been to their home before, and when I arrive, I sit in the car for a few minutes, surveying the bird feeders scattered across their lawn and double-checking the time to make sure I'm not early. Finally, I take a deep breath and walk up the driveway. Mark answers the door of the modest suburban split-level, ushering me into the foyer and introducing me to Eli, the family's placid black lab. Mark explains that Lesley is out driving with their daughter Kate, who is not quite sixteen, in effort to log a few hours toward her license. "She'll be back any minute," he promises, excusing himself to give Lesley a call.

I sit at the kitchen island, waiting. It's quiet here. Peaceful. Mark and Lesley's three boys are grown now, living on their own, and what remains is a smaller, presumably calmer version of what once was.

Mark returns to report that Lesley and Kate are on their way. He pours me a glass of water and we chat about teenagers and the perils of learning to drive in congested DC traffic. The front door opens, and Mark greets Lesley with a warm smile and helps her transfer a large batch of white chicken chili from a leaking slow-cooker to a Dutch oven. "You wanted to write about our real lives," he laughs, wiping up the spilled chili, "here you go!"

Kate vanishes upstairs, and we sit down in the living room to talk, Eli sprawled across the hardwood floor between Mark and Lesley's seats. I settle back into the overstuffed chair they insist I use and ask them to start at the beginning, to tell me how they met and how they came to identify themselves as Christians. I want to know about their stillbirth, about the daughter they lost, but I also want to know about them, the kind of people they are, the way their suffering fits into the larger story of their lives.

Lesley speaks first. "We met as freshmen in our college dorm. We were both seventeen." "Our first date was a Grateful Dead concert in San Francisco," Mark adds.

I've heard Mark tell this story before, perhaps in a sermon, but it's a delightful scene to imagine. There's nothing about Mark and Lesley that suggests Grateful Dead fans. They're quiet and conservative, mature, respectable parents of young adults. Their house is decorated with Oriental rugs and watercolors. It's hard to imagine them as teenagers in the seventies, harder still to picture them singing along with Jerry Garcia.

"We didn't smoke any pot or anything," Mark continues. "We were just there sort of being good and not taking drugs, but we were there." They both laugh.

Lesley explains that they dated through college, during their time together at Humboldt State University in Northern California, as well as the year she spent studying abroad in Sweden.

"It was brutal," Mark says of being apart from Lesley for that year, and even now, more than three decades later, his gaze on his wife lingers—their affection palpable.

College is when they fell in love, but college, I learn, is also when they fell in love with Jesus. Both came into school professing to be Christians, but both now believe they lacked an understanding of what that actually meant. "I was very worldly and very proud and arrogant," Mark admits.

"I was never really challenged with the gospel . . . or really aware of the gospel," Lesley says.

They figured it out together, walking arm-in-arm toward God and toward the local church. After positive experiences with the campus ministries Intervarsity and the Navigators, they both became involved with a little Baptist church along the edge of campus. They married in 1982, six years after they met, and settled down in Arcata, a tiny college town bordering the university. It was a town with an interesting mixture of academics, students, and blue-collar workers. The main industries in Arcata at the time, Mark reports, were "logging, fishing, and marijuana growing. Probably not in that order."

It was there in early 1985, in the small, two-bedroom house they shared, that they learned they were expecting their first child. "We'd waited a few years," Mark says. "We thought we were ready. And it was a pretty big deal because it would have been the first grandchild for both sets of grandparents."

Kate comes down the steps, dressed for a run. Eli springs up, ready to join her. Mark and Lesley tell them goodbye, then continue their story.

The pregnancy progressed normally, and they were busy planning for a move to Pasadena, California shortly after the baby's October due date. Mark, feeling God was calling him to leave behind his dreams of a forestry career and pursue full-time pastoral ministry, had been accepted to Fuller Theological Seminary and planned to start classes there in January of 1986.

Neither Mark nor Lesley remembers much about the pregnancy itself. "I've subsequently had four more pregnancies, so they do kind of run together," Lesley muses.

"A long time ago," Mark agrees, his voice quiet and slow.

But they do remember the August 5 appointment with their obstetrician. It was a normal day, a routine checkup. Their baby was thirty-two weeks, nearly full-term. Only two months to go. "We just went in with no idea that there was anything wrong," Lesley says.

Mark happened to be accompanying Lesley that day. "I wanted to be there," he explains. "I just felt this excitement, probably a combination of excitement and responsibility."

In the mid-1980s, ultrasound was not the routine procedure it is for many pregnant patients today, so the OB used only a stethoscope to detect the baby's heartbeat. Mark remembers the doctor's words clearly. "He said, 'I can't hear a heartbeat. This is serious, and we need to do an ultrasound.'"

The ultrasound confirmed their fears: their baby had died, most likely in the previous few days.

"I'd never been pregnant before," Lesley explains. "I didn't know the signs, like that there was no movement or anything."

Mark continues, "It wasn't until they started asking you questions did you realize, 'Oh yeah the last couple days . . .'" He trails off.

"Seems like [the baby's] been kind of quiet," Lesley finishes for him. She pauses, and I think back to my own appointment when there was no heartbeat. In retrospect, I too recognized signs I'd missed at first.

The hardest part, they agree, is that it was a Friday afternoon, too late to begin an induction. They were admitted to a nearby hospital to spend the night, anticipating the delivery of their baby the following day, a delivery that was suddenly so different from the one they'd been preparing for. Mark recalls, "That was probably the hardest night of our lives . . . just knowing that's coming but having to wait."

Lesley nods. "You just can't believe." She recalls thinking, "*Maybe they made a mistake. Is there any way this could be wrong?*" She prayed that somehow, miraculously, the baby would live.

Mark felt a visceral urge to escape. "The way I processed this was, okay, this is really bad, and this baby's dead. We just need to get out of this and get away from here . . . If we could have suddenly snapped our fingers and made it all go away and then gone home, I would have taken that."

Reeling, Mark managed to make the necessary phone calls to their parents and, he thinks but can't be certain, to their pastor. He remembers his dad asking if they should make the six-hour drive north from San Mateo, California. Mark isn't sure if he told him no or was merely indifferent, but he knows he didn't beg his parents to come. "I didn't realize how much I needed people," he says. "I was just overwhelmed with this grief, and I probably wouldn't have even used the word 'grief.' I was just overwhelmed with emotion."

But then a few things happened that caused him to reevaluate his initial impulses. First, he began to read through a small booklet the hospital provided, which described some of the decisions the couple would have to face the following day: Would they hold the baby? Give it a name? Have a funeral? The booklet, shares Mark, "slowly helped me realize this isn't a problem we solve by pushing it away from us. This is our baby, and we're only going to get one chance here. I started to realize if we don't hold the baby and look at the baby, we're going to regret this for the rest of our lives."

Second, even though they hadn't asked him to, Mark and Lesley's pastor Charles came to the hospital to spend time with them. They had never known until that night, but Charles and his wife had also endured the early death of a baby, their firstborn, whose severe birth defects had allowed only a very short life.

"What I remember about Charles was that he did just the right thing," Mark says, his voice wavering and his eyes filling with tears. "He just came. He didn't come to do a Bible study. He didn't come to tell his story. He just came."

Sitting in the Mullerys's living room, I start to cry as well, thinking of all the people who "just came" when Avaleen died and of how much their presence meant to us. I think too of Mark and Lesley's carefully worded emails in the days after we shared news of our loss.

Mark goes on to explain that somehow, between the hospital booklet, the visit from Charles, and the compassion of their obstetrician, his whole orientation to their situation changed. "The Lord used the pain of us having to wait that night," he says. "It could have all happened right away. I would have made all those decisions based on where my starting points were, and my starting points were all wrong."

For Mark, this was the first evidence that even in such a terrible tragedy, God was both present and at work, leading them and carrying them through their haze of grief.

"What do you remember, Lesley?" I ask, my tone gentle. I'm struck by how vividly Mark remembers that night and how articulately he's able to describe it, and I wonder if Lesley's experience was similar.

"I was a little out of it, I think," she says, explaining that she'd been given some medication to help her sleep. "And I'm more of a responder. I just felt like this is our baby; it's good that we hold her." She recalls being more focused on how she was going to handle the impending delivery.

As she talks, I realize that Lesley is like CJ, steadfast and focused on what needs to be done, while I am more like Mark, reflective and introspective about my experiences.

Though they remember that difficult night differently, Mark and Lesley faced the morning of August 6, 1985 together. That day, Lesley was induced and then delivered their baby, a little girl. She weighed three pounds, fifteen and a half ounces. They saw her. They held her. They named her Sarah.

And then they walked out of the hospital and went home alone. Lesley shares her deep sadness. "I went through this whole period of kind of grieving what I didn't get," she says. "The baby never came home, and it felt very empty and sad. There's nothing you can do; there's just no baby."

The front door opens. Kate and Eli are back from their run. Kate goes back upstairs to her room, but Eli moseys into the living room to join us. "Hi Eli," says Mark, patting the dog's head.

Both Mark and Lesley remember how hard it was for them to tell other people what had happened. Lesley recalls a particular incident at a post office she frequented regularly as part of her job. During her pregnancy, the women at the post office had always asked her how the baby was doing, and when she showed up for the first time after the stillbirth, obviously no longer pregnant, the employees asked if she'd had the baby. "I just kind of ran out," Lesley says, explaining that she was "totally emotionally not ready for that."

For the Mullerys, though, the anguish of that time did not push them away from God. "You have to turn to God," Lesley says. She pauses and corrects herself. "You don't have to, but you can choose to see that God is good and He's enough."

"There's always enough in God," Mark asserts. "There's more in God than our loss or our unanswerable or unanswered questions or just the agony of the pain and the grief of the emotions or the physical experiences. Just like grace goes deeper than sin . . . there's always more in Him than what we lack or how much we hurt. That's what leads us to worship."

I nod. I like the sound of what he is saying, the idea of God being bigger than our pain and our questions. I want to believe in this kind of God. And yet, as I listen to Mark talk, I have to admit that I'm not certain I do. The ache inside me demands to be filled, and the questions I carry scream for answers, and so I wonder: *Is God really enough for this?*

Mark and Lesley go on to describe the funeral they held for Sarah. Mark's parents came, as well as Charles and some friends from their church. The couple chose a few words to inscribe on Sarah's headstone to serve as a reminder that even though her life was short, Sarah was formed by God in His image. The words came from Ps 139:14b, *Wonderful are your works.*

At first, this verse unsettles me. I understand the Mullerys chose it because they believe their daughter's life, brief as it was, was designed by God with beauty and dignity. I believe that too, both of Sarah and of my own Avaleen. But if their short lives were a wonderful work of God, I reason, then their deaths must be too. If God is sovereign over all things, as Scripture seems to suggest, then both life and death are in His hands. Therefore, He either directly willed or at the very least permitted through this will Sarah and Avaleen to die. The thought is difficult for me to embrace. Mark admits it wasn't a simple conclusion for them either, that it "took awhile to get to *wonderful are your works.*"

But even as one part of my brain fights against this acknowledgement of God's sovereignty, another part of me does understand. From the beginning, even though her presence inside me made me ill for months, even though her loss has created the deepest hurt I've ever known, I have always been thankful for Avaleen's life. I've never wished that she hadn't existed at all; in fact, many times I've wished she lived longer, that if she had to die young, CJ and I might have been allowed a few brief moments to hold and kiss her. I know this would have only made my sorrow more profound, but I wish for a longer life, more of her.

Still. *Wonderful are your works?* It rolled off my tongue when Ellie was a fresh newborn, when life was a sweet, breathtaking miracle. But when Avaleen died, was God doing a wonderful work then too? He was there in the darkest moments, caring for our family in our sadness, even changing us for the better through our suffering. But I simply can't understand why God would take her. And I don't expect I ever will.

Lesley verbalizes a similar thought. "We just can't understand what God's doing here," she says. "We can try, but we're not going to ever figure this out. But we do know that God is good and that His works are good."

I can tell the Mullerys really believe this, that though there are tears for both of them all these years later, they have a deep faith that God is good in all things, including the death of their daughter. They can trace God's real and tender hand in the events surrounding Sarah's death—the presence of a compassionate obstetrician, the unsolicited visit from their pastor, the long, painful night that helped Mark choose to hold his baby girl.

And though they do not understand why Sarah had to die, they can see glimpses of God at work in and through their suffering. "There was a foundation laid there for our marriage," Lesley says.

"Thanks for saying that," Mark says, his voice husky. He looks directly at Lesley. "Yeah, I can remember we talked a lot about . . . how [our loss] knit us together in ways that were very sweet." There is a long and intimate silence between them.

"It humbled us," Mark finally says.

"It was very humbling," Lesley echoes.

Mark goes on, "I think we've too tightly connected humility with sin, but in the Bible, humility is more than that because otherwise how could Jesus be humble? Humility is dependence, and I think that's a really important reality. This experience . . . humbled us in the sense that it made us smaller and made God bigger and drew us near to Him in light of that."

He recounts the Bible story of Job, who in brief succession lost his property, his possessions, his children, his health, and the respect of his friends, a suffering beyond anything I have experienced or can imagine. Mark narrows in on Job 42:5–6, verses from the very last chapter, verses he has no way of knowing were particularly significant to me in the year we struggled to get pregnant for the first time. In them, Job, who has spent nearly forty chapters wrestling in conversation with his friends and with God as he tries to understand and explain his suffering and to find God in those experiences, finally surrenders: *I had heard of you by the hearing of the ear,* he says, *but now my eye sees you; therefore I despise myself, and repent in dust and ashes.*

What drew me to those verses is the way they show that Job's suffering helped him see God in a way he hadn't before, even though he's described from the beginning as a holy and righteous man. While we waited to get pregnant with Ellie, I often thought about this passage and prayed that my pain would somehow help me know God more deeply. Today, however, Mark narrows in on another aspect of these verses, pointing out something I haven't ever considered. "This quest to get . . . God in a box, to question him as a defendant, that's what he's repenting of," Mark says. "He's saying, 'No I'm not going to make understanding everything that's happening to me the point of contingency for worship.'"

His words sting. He's right, but I also know how hard it is to let go of the quest to understand. Part of my reason for doing this interview, for writing this book in the first place, is that I want to understand, to find glimpses of what God might be up to. Listening to Mark and Lesley makes me realize that I've been hoping to find in other people's stories the explanations and clarity about God's purposes that elude me in my own. But already, one interview in, I'm reminded God does not promise we will understand His every move.

For Mark and Lesley, this is a lesson they learned not only through their experience of stillbirth, but also when their second child, Peter, was diagnosed with leukemia at eighteen months, just three years after Sarah's death. Mark was a pastor by then, and he recalls walking onto stage one Sunday morning shortly after learning of Peter's cancer, while a song called "In the Presence of a Holy God" was playing. I know the song, though I haven't heard it in years. It begins, *In the presence of a holy God, I bow down and I adore.*[3]

3. Altrogge, "In the Presence," lines 1-2.

Mark remembers listening to the words and thinking, *"Am I going to do it or not? Am I still going to do that if two children die?"* Across from me in the living room, his eyes fill with tears. "Yeah, I'm going to do that. What else can I do? Why wouldn't I? He's the Lord . . . There was a sense of the glory and the holiness and greatness of God in the midst of the agony of pain and questions that can't be answered."

I know the end of Peter's story; I've seen his tousled mop of sand-colored hair and his wide smile from across the sanctuary on multiple Sundays. But I think of what Mark and Lesley must have felt in those days, knowing the horror of losing one child, fearful of losing another. And in the days and weeks that follow, I keep coming back to this moment Mark has described, the moment where he chose to worship in the midst of suffering. I keep thinking about what it means to worship when we do not understand, wondering how praise can coexist with a broken heart.

———

The Sunday following our interview, my basal body temperature plummets. I've been charting my cycle long enough by now to be certain of what this means: we haven't gotten pregnant on our first attempt post-miscarriage. I feel disappointed and a bit betrayed. I know it's bad theology, but I've thought multiple times that, after all we've been through in losing Avaleen and in the draining months of tests and medical procedures after her death, God should make it easy for us to have another child, like perhaps we're owed that small consolation. And now, the dreams I've been allowing to grow inside of me unravel. Another month without a baby.

I stand in church that morning, surrounded by people who seem to be praising God with ease, and struggle to even open my mouth. I look over at Mark and Lesley in the front row of the sanctuary, singing in agreement with the words of the song: *Behold our God, seated on His throne, come let us adore Him.*[4] I think of Mark all those years ago, choosing to sing with one child in the grave and one child in the hospital fighting for his life. And I think, *Oh man. I have to do this. I have to sing, even with one baby lost, the hope of another denied.* The tears roll down my face, but I sing. I sing the words and pray that one I day I will feel the full weight of their truth again. I try to let go of my need to understand God. I try to remember that God is here and present in my pain. I try to worship.

4. Baird, Baird, Altrogge, and Baird, "Behold Our God," lines 5–6.

God, help me to trust You and Your goodness and care for me in this suffering and waiting and confusion. I do not understand. I am hurting. I feel alone. I feel scared. God, help me to see that You are here, with me, right now in all of this . . . Give me peace.

—JOURNAL ENTRY, FEBRUARY 13, 2013

Chapter 5

FEBRUARY: BRIAN AND LINDA

I arrange the silverware on the table just so and smooth out the wrinkles in the tablecloth one last time. Guests will arrive soon for the baby shower I'm hosting tonight, a celebration for a friend from church who's expecting her second child in a few weeks. Her daughter is exactly two months younger than Ellie, and we've gotten to know one another over the past few years, chatting during playdates about breastfeeding woes and language acquisition and teaching our girls to share their baby dolls and dress-up clothes.

It feels strange that she's about to have her second child and I'm not even pregnant. *You do have a second child*, I remind myself, *and it's not a competition.*

I remember Becca's words from a few days ago. "I know you've only been trying for one month," she'd told me when I mentioned how much I was struggling. "But it feels like so much longer."

And she's right, I think, as I use clothespins to hang tiny onesies on a piece of twine strung across a bookshelf. It's been almost a full year since Avaleen was conceived, and the past twelve months have been long, filled with grief and endless doctor's appointments and hour after interminable hour on the phone with the insurance company. We've been trying for one month, but the journey to another baby feels like it began a long time ago.

———

This month, I'm scheduled to interview Brian and Linda Johnson, a couple in our church small group. Shortly before CJ and I were married in 2008, we bought a townhome on a street adjacent to theirs and became neighbors. A year or two later, Brian and Linda and their two children joined the small group that meets in our home, and we became friends.

It's hard not to like Brian and Linda. They're smart and engaging, both genuine. Brian, an intelligence analyst with a PhD in International Politics and Strategic Studies, teaches strategic intelligence classes at a local Christian college. He's one of those rare readers and thinkers who can engage not only his fellow book lovers and history buffs, but also the sports fanatics, awkward tweens, and shy two year olds who frequent our small group. Linda, a former elementary school teacher, is energetic and organized, adept at managing her busy little ones. She sits rarely, walks briskly, talks freely, and laughs easily.

At four and a half and newly three, Anika and Tristan are a pleasure to observe and interact with but, like most preschoolers, are not always the easiest to parent. In other words, they are delightful, demanding, normal, crazy, wonderful children. Anika is creative, a natural performer, highly verbal, a lover of pink and musicals and babies and dancing. Tristan is quieter, more content to play on his own, absorbed by his trains. In his more social moments, he boasts a winning smile and a fantastic sense of humor.

On the Friday night of our interview, I walk down the street to their house. It's only a block away, but the wind is cold and I walk fast, pulling the hood of my puffy jacket around my face. My lungs are burning by the time I arrive. Linda greets me at the door and invites me in. Anika and Tristan are fast asleep upstairs, so we chat while she finishes sweeping her kitchen floor. "I used to be able to do this once a week," she laughs, brushing an impressive pile of crumbs into the trash can. "With kids, it's an everyday project!"

Brian enters, and we seat ourselves around the living room on furniture upholstered in floral print, surrounded by a toy piano, dress-up clothes, and an impressive array of board books. Linda, who's originally from Britain, pours us steaming mugs of tea. We begin to talk.

Brian grew up in a family of nominal faith, his father Catholic, his mother Lutheran. He attended a variety of churches over the years, some with his parents, some with friends: Lutheran, Charismatic, Baptist. He was, as he puts it, "an evangelical mongrel."

Eventually, after his parents' divorce, Brian's church involvement mostly ceased. "I wouldn't say I really had much of a faith," he says. "If I was dating somebody who went to church, I would go to church."

Over the years, he responded to numerous altar calls. However, Brian's life didn't really change until the summer before his freshmen year of college, when he heard a sermon about not mocking God and realized he needed to take his faith more seriously. "That is the point where I understood what the gospel was," he explains.

For Linda, whose Dad is an ordained Anglican minister and whose parents had spent their lives as missionaries and working for various missions organizations, church was a much more regular and consistent part of life. When she was eleven, she attended a Billy Graham crusade meeting her father was helping to organize and was confronted for the first time with the thought that her faith needed to be her own. "I think that was the moment of realizing that my parents' faith wasn't mine and wasn't going to be mine unless there was some act on—" She pauses, realizing she's talked herself into a tricky theological question. "Well, act on God's part, my part, you know." She laughs.

Though their church backgrounds were different, both Brian and Linda describe their college years as pivotal to their spiritual development. They met in the co-ed bathroom of their dorm the first Sunday of Linda's freshmen year at the University of California-Santa Cruz. Brian, a senior, was either brushing his teeth or combing his hair (neither of them can remember exactly), when Linda walked in, aware that it was a Sunday morning, but having no idea exactly how to get to church. Brian happened to mention that he and his roommate were headed to a service and invited Linda to join them. She did.

They weren't really interested in each other at first. "He looked like Shaggy from *Scooby Doo*," Linda says. But as it turned out, they were next-door neighbors, and between Linda borrowing Brian's phone to call home and their joint participation in the campus's Intervarsity group, they quickly developed a friendship. By Christmas, when Linda's parents drove them to their respective homes in Southern California, there was a definite attraction on both sides.

"Then the torment of your soul began," Linda says, laughing.

"Yes," Brian nods. He wasn't sure if it was fair to start dating Linda, knowing he was graduating soon and that he was probably headed overseas for at least a year with Intervarsity. And there was that pesky fact that she was so young.

"I was still only seventeen," Linda explains.

Brian spent months waffling. Finally, on a road trip with his room-mate to visit Brian's dad in Idaho, the roommate lost it. "He said, 'I don't want to hear this anymore,'" Brian recounts, "'if you love her, tell her. Okay? Don't talk to me about it. Just tell her.'"

Brian did, and he and Linda have been together since, though much of their early relationship was long-distance. Brian spent a year in the former Soviet Union doing missionary work, and then a year and a half after that working and taking master's classes in Southern California while Linda finished her undergraduate schooling. During the time they did have together, they bonded over their shared love of history. "We had what we called going on dates," Linda explains. "We actually never really went on many dates because, you know, we were students. So we would actually sit on the front porch and come up with dates in history. Brian [would say] 1732, and I had to come up with something that happened in 1732. And we'd go back and forth."

I smile, treasuring the wonderful nerdiness of this. I'd be hopelessly useless at this sort of "dating," but on another level, I can relate—CJ and I spent many of our pre-marriage dates in coffee shops working on our respective grad school assignments.

Brian and Linda married when Linda finished school, at ages twenty-four and twenty, respectively. Both had dreams of children, with Brian picturing two and Linda planning for what she considered the ideal number of five. "I didn't want four because that was like my family, and six was too much like *The Brady Bunch*. Three's an odd number, and I think I had even figured out multi-packs of potato chips came in so many . . ." She chuckles, never finishing her sentence and leaving me to contemplate how the number of potato chips in a multi-pack could lead one to determine that five is the perfect number of children.

They both intended to add children to their family while they were young, but as Brian pursued first a master's degree and then a PhD, they put starting a family on hold so Linda could provide a steady source of income. Finally, eight years into marriage, as Brian neared the end of his dissertation process, they decided they were ready to start trying. Linda, always a planner, was trying to schedule a pregnancy in conjunction with her summer break from teaching. "Okay if I get pregnant this month," she says, describing her reasoning at the time, "then I have the baby in April, then I could have my maternity leave for ten weeks, and then it will be the end of the school year."

But she didn't have a baby that April. Or the next. Four years passed, and still Linda wasn't pregnant.

"Wasn't that super challenging for you?" I ask, marveling that Brian and Linda were content to wait all those years before even beginning to try for children and that four years of infertility didn't seem to faze them.

"Not for me," Linda says, taking another sip of tea.

Brian agrees. "No . . . I can't remember feeling apprehensive or anxious or worried at that point."

I'm struck by how pessimistic I am in contrast. I started to worry when I couldn't get pregnant the first time. By six months, I was convinced something was seriously wrong. Even now, after just one failed attempt at a third pregnancy, I've started researching possible causes and treatments for sub-par fertility.

For Brian and Linda, though, it wasn't until they relocated from California to Virginia in January of 2005 that they really began to struggle. As they met people in their new church—the church we're all members of now—they remember countless awkward conversations during which people asked how long they'd been married and if they had any children. When the Johnsons said they did not, "there'd be this sort of a pause for a moment," Linda recalls. "It was almost like, *So you're Christians and you've been married eleven years and you don't have any kids?* So then you start feeling like maybe we are a little weird."

Even then, they were not particularly concerned about their prospects for having children. "I was sort of in fix-it mode," Linda explains. She read *Taking Charge of Your Fertility*, a book I also read when we were trying to get pregnant with Ellie, and charted her cycles more carefully, convinced "it could work itself out."

However, by fall of 2006, after having tried on their own for five plus years, Brian and Linda finally decided it was time for infertility testing. All of their results came back normal except for one: Linda's hormone levels revealed advanced ovarian aging. The doctor said it was highly unlikely the Johnsons would ever conceive a child and recommended they try in vitro fertilization (IVF). But the couple had known, even prior to testing, that they weren't really interested in IVF. The Johnsons were concerned about ethical issues like selective reduction and unused fertilized embryos, as well as pouring a lot of money into a procedure which offered no guarantee.

"Here's the stone tablet," says Linda, describing the moment the doctor presented IVF as their only hope. "The gate has closed."

"Christmas Eve that year was very, very hard," Brian says. Still reeling from the diagnosis as the holiday neared, they'd been asked to help serve refreshments following our church's Christmas Eve service. Cleaning up afterward, "everyone was pretty much gone, and we were the only people left in the kitchen," Linda recalls. "We were washing the big coffee pots, and it's like nine o'clock on Christmas Eve . . . and we're realizing we're here because we have no kids. Nobody with kids is here because they're home with their kids."

"And you wonder if this is what it's going to be like for the rest of our lives," Brian adds. "Is this what we can expect?"

While they grieved the loss of the biological children they'd long desired, Brian and Linda still wanted to grow their family. Brian describes his sense of urgency: "We can't take too much time because at some point we're going to reach the point where we won't have any time."

Having ruled out IVF, he and Linda began to pursue adoption. At first, they expected to adopt internationally, like some of their friends, but as they did more research, they began to strongly consider a domestic adoption. "I wanted to be a mother for the whole life of my child," Linda says, explaining that many international adoptions occur when the child is no longer a newborn, and often when they're no longer an infant.

Brian worried, though, about the close proximity and involvement of birth mothers and birth families. "I was very scared . . . about domestic adoption."

"I don't remember being excited at this point, to be honest," Linda agrees. "It was more just kind of moving forward . . . if we want a family, this is what we need to do."

I appreciate their honesty. I've always thought of adoption as a beautiful thing, a thing I'd like to be able to do some day, but I've also felt fearful of the risk and uncertainty. I've wondered recently if the fertility difficulties CJ and I have experienced are somehow hints from God that we're supposed to adopt, but so many of the people I know who've adopted seem, at least from my distance, to have entered into it without significant apprehension or struggle. Listening to Brian and Linda, I realize it doesn't have to be that way. For the first time, I feel released to consider adoption without the pressure of feeling confident excitement from the outset.

Brian and Linda faced other challenges as they moved forward. Linda's extended family is diverse, and she and Brian knew they had love to offer a child of any racial or ethnic background. Still, they wrestled with the implications of this choice, wondering exactly what it would look like to advocate for and support a child of a different race. Brian explains, "It brings up a host of challenges regarding how to prepare a child to confront existing stereotypes [and] how to feel connected to their community of origin."

And then there was the paperwork, including an extensive list of medical conditions they had to decide whether or not they would accept in a prospective child. Brian and Linda tried to make decisions based on what their income would support or what their townhome could accommodate, but they found the process difficult. "You almost feel like you're valuing somebody," Linda says. "It's horrible . . . questions nobody should be asked to answer."

Spiritually, it was hard for the Johnsons to see God in all of this. First of all, Brian says, "We're in a church that is filled with kids, filled to the brim with children."

"Everywhere you look there's children oozing out of every hole," Linda continues. I smile, knowing exactly how empty it feels to sit in our church on a Sunday morning, childless.

"It was very difficult to listen to testimonies where [the situation] worked out in the end. On any topic," Brian says. "It's great to hear that, and I know intellectually I'm supposed to be encouraged . . . but there's no guarantee that this is going to work out."

I often feel this way when CJ tells me everything will be fine, that I don't need to worry. There's a good chance he's right, but there's also no way he can know for sure. Following God does not guarantee a happy ending, at least on this side of eternity, and sometimes, the stories of other people's happy endings, as inspiring as they should be, are reminders of our own unresolved pain.

The Johnsons continued to wrestle with these difficult emotions as they proceeded with their adoption, completing their paperwork in April of 2008. They expected it would take another six to twelve months before they'd be matched with a baby, and that even if they were chosen by birth parents right away, it would be a few months until their baby was born.

Far as the Curse Is Found

"Chances are the baby wouldn't be born until June, so I'd finish the school year," Linda explains.

"You were still planning around the school year!" I'm teasing her, but truth be told, I'd probably have done the same thing. We all laugh.

"My plan was summertime," Linda continues, "I'm going to start working on the nursery, thinking about stuff I need."

Instead, weeks after submitting their paperwork, the Johnsons received a call from their social worker notifying them that a highly unlikely scenario had occurred: they'd already been selected by a birth parent whose baby had just been born. They could meet the little girl the next day, a Saturday, and take her home a few days later.

"Then it moves from kind of theoretical to practical realism and shock," Brian says, "because we're not ready."

Though they felt unprepared, the Johnsons decided to proceed and went to meet the baby at the home of her temporary caregivers. The experience was strange, Linda recalls. "I was thinking this could be my baby but then . . . you feel like you're going to visit somebody else . . ."

". . . who just had their baby?" I offer after she trails off.

"Right."

"Very surreal," Brian adds. "But . . . it was *yes*. This is what we want to do. This is who we want as our child."

Friends from church lent the Johnsons baby equipment and clothes, and they made a run to Target for the essentials: diapers, formula, a pack and play. There, in the parking lot, right beside the second cart return, they chose a name for their new daughter: Anika Destiny. Destiny was the name the birth mother had selected for her baby, and the Johnsons chose to keep it as a middle name. Anika means "sweet face," and they thought it captured their daughter well. "Babies can look pretty weird," Linda laughs. "Tristan was like a strange little elf man, but she had this very beautiful face even as a young baby."

And then, just like that, they brought her home. Anika was eight days old at the time, and there were two days remaining until the birth mother relinquished her rights, then another twenty until the birth father's were terminated. The Johnsons feared having to give Anika back; at first, they were unsure how to feel. Linda says she was tempted to think, "*I don't want to love this child yet because I don't know.*"

"You can't do it," Brian interjects. "You can't approach it that way."

Linda agrees, "God has put this baby in my home to be loved for as long as [she's] here, and that's true for anyone's kids."

I nod in agreement, thinking of how loving Avaleen for the three short months she lived inside me had ended up breaking my heart, but also of how I would do it all over again.

The Johnsons threw themselves wholeheartedly into loving Anika. They made excited phone calls to aunts, uncles, and grandparents. They tried to figure out how to handle Anika's congested breathing and keep her comfortable in spite of a broken air conditioner.

Linda remembers thinking, "*Oh my goodness! We're going to break her.*"

I smile, thinking how similar their first few days as parents were to our own: excitement, confusion, the fearful responsibility of caring for a completely helpless child. I hadn't known Brian and Linda well in those days, but I'm reminded of the first time I saw them with Anika. CJ and I were walking on a path in the woods behind the Johnsons's home one evening and happened upon them pushing Anika in her stroller. I was struck then by the beautiful contrasts: Brian with his crew cut and flannel shirt, Linda with her neat bun and British accent, both of them tall, pale. And then there was their tiny, brown daughter and her sweet, round face.

My phone vibrates, a text from CJ appearing: *Where are you?*

I realize we've been talking for nearly two hours, but the Johnsons haven't finished their story, and there are still multiple questions on my list. I send my reply: *I'll try to be home by eleven!*

For the Johnsons, weeks quickly turned into months, and eventually, Anika's adoption was finalized. Brian and Linda spent the first year of her life absorbed in learning how to become her parents. In the backs of their minds, they expected to adopt again, another African-American child, probably around the time Anika turned three.

But then in the summer of 2009, Linda noticed it had been an especially long time since her last period. "I remember thinking, basically there's one of two options here. Either this is menopause beginning, or I'm pregnant." Because she'd been diagnosed with advanced ovarian aging, Linda assumed the former, but since "they don't really make a menopause test," she reasons, she bought a pregnancy test instead.

It was positive. "I was staring at the sink, looking at the directions," Linda says, thinking: "*What am I going to do? I haven't planned for this, and Anika's only one.*"

"Shock," says Brian, simply and seriously.

Though they were excited about being able to have a biological child and about no longer being excluded from the experience of pregnancy, there were challenges wrapped up in this situation for the Johnsons. In particular, since Brian was now forty and Linda was in her mid-thirties, they had planned to adopt only one more child. Now that their second would be biological, they were concerned Anika would lose the opportunity to have a sibling who looked like her. "'This one's going to be a blonde-haired, blue-eyed, fair child, which is going to make her more the odd one out," Linda says. She wondered, "*Is this going to contribute to her alienation at some point?*"

They struggled, too, with the way others responded to their news. Again and again, people told them that families who adopt due to infertility always end up getting pregnant shortly thereafter. "You hear all these stories," Brian says, "but the percentage is actually rather low." In fact, I learn later, The National Infertility Association reports a couple's odds of getting pregnant are exactly the same, whether or not they adopt.[5]

People also regularly told Brian and Linda how glad they were that God answered their prayers. "Oh, you did something good by adopting," Brian says, describing the implication behind these comments, "therefore God answered your prayer."

"And gave you a pregnancy," Linda clarifies.

The Johnsons feel this way of thinking minimizes not only the precious gift of Anika but also God's faithfulness in the story of her adoption. "God answered our prayer . . . the first time around," Brian explains. "There wasn't this transactional thing going on."

As Brian and Linda look back on their story of building a family, a story that took them through years of infertility, adoption, and then pregnancy, they see God's hand in all of it.

"God answered our prayer for children with Anika," Brian says. "That's how God answered that prayer. And then He answered it again with Tristan. But why He chose to do it that way, I can't answer. I don't know. But it was right and it was good and it was wonderful."

Brian recalls an article he read by theologian Mirsolav Volf, who suffered through nine years of infertility with his wife.[6] In the article, Volf

5. RESOLVE: The National Infertility Association, "Myths and Facts about Infertility," lines 19–20.

6. Volf, "The Gift of Infertility," 33.

begins by calling infertility a curse, but then ends by recognizing it's also a gift because it led him to his two adopted sons.

"If there hadn't been infertility," Brian says, referring to Volf's perspective as well as his own, "I wouldn't have the family I have now."

Brian acknowledges that if they'd been able to conceive children as planned, they would have had a different family, one they'd presumably love just as much. But, he believes, "with God, there isn't an alternative reality." The story we live is *the* story God wrote for us.

Linda came to a similar conclusion during a seminar for perspective parents early in their adoption process. Up until that point, she shares, "It sort of felt like we couldn't have our own children, so I guess we'll just have to adopt somebody else's." But the seminar emphasized God's sovereignty and the fact that "God doesn't have a Plan B for building families." For Linda, it was helpful to realize that "infertility might be a surprise to us, but it's not to God."

"And you just don't have any control. You don't," Brian says.

"*The heart of man plans his way, but the Lord establishes his steps,*" Linda adds, quoting the familiar words of Prov 16:9. "As somebody who's a planner, it's hard when you have no clue."

"I put Anika to bed last night," Brian says, "and we've been having these conversations. She wants to hear about what it was like growing up in Idaho, so we talk about those things . . . She fell asleep yesterday, and I sat and watched her for a little while . . . and I can't picture having a different daughter. I can't." He pauses. "But again, there's no control over that."

No control. A phrase I've thought of often in conjunction with infertility and miscarriage. To be sure, there are things you can do when you're hoping to conceive and birth healthy children: chart your cycles, have lots of sex, eat healthy foods, and avoid alcohol and smoking. But really, ultimately, life is not in your hands. For people like the Johnsons and myself— like most of us, really—who like to plan and control the course of our lives, this often feels like a harsh reality.

The story of my family has certainly not gone according to plan. My plan didn't include waiting a year to get pregnant or never getting to meet my second child. It didn't include the waiting we're currently facing as we try to get pregnant again. And yet, I understand Brian's point. In spite of my broken plans, God has answered our prayers. He gave us Ellie, and I simply can't imagine any other daughter. She is well worth the wait.

It's harder to think about Avaleen's death in this light. Seeing redemption in waiting is one thing; seeing redemption in death is quite another. Even if we go on to have five more children, there will always be a hole in our family where Avaleen should be. I'll always miss the particular child she was, grieve that I never got to know her, that Ellie will not grow up with the sister she wouldn't have been able to remember ever being without.

But there is mysterious resonance here too. After our miscarriage, my dad wrote me a card expressing his care and sympathy. In it, he recalled how he and my mom had lost their first child in an early miscarriage just months before conceiving me, and then he went on to explain something I'd never considered before: *If that child had been born, you Abby, would never have graced our lives. There is mystery in God's ways and sovereignty that we will never understand. But this loss in that mysteriousness of God will result in untold blessing and joy.* That's just it. We cannot understand. We cannot control. But as my dad wrote, God works in and through suffering to bring mysterious joy.

———

A few days after my interview with the Johnsons, around the same time I learn we aren't pregnant this month either, Brian emails me a link to the Miroslav Volf article he referenced. I read it and am struck by one line in particular about Volf's view of his own children in light of his wife's infertility: *Since it gave me what I now can't imagine living without, poison was transmuted into a gift, God's strange gift. The pain of it remains, of course. But the poison is gone.*[7]

I think again of the Johnsons and their story. I think of the pain that lingers, of how they wish they were younger, worry their own parents are too old to play an active role in their children's lives, fear they won't live long enough to meet their own grandchildren. I think of Anika and of how aware she is already of the color of her skin, of how it must have been hard for her birth mother to let her go. There is still very real pain here.

But it is true that some of the poison is gone. Brian and Linda don't have to wash coffee pots on Christmas Eve, wondering if it will ever be more than the two of them. Anika will grow up knowing she is a loved and chosen member of the Johnson family. God has answered prayers and woven redeeming touches.

7. Ibid., 33.

I don't know yet how the story of our family will turn out. Perhaps, like my parents, CJ and I will soon conceive a child who wouldn't have existed had Avaleen lived. Perhaps, like the Johnsons, we will adopt. Perhaps God will lead us down another path all our own. It helps, though, in this season of not knowing, when the poisons of grief and loneliness remain present and strong, to be reminded that God wins, that redemption triumphs, that there will be a day, in eternity if not now, when we will see clearly that all of this struggle and loss was indeed somehow God's strange and mysterious gift.

We're in a sweet spot, our tiny family of three. I try to remember this even as I feel the gap where your sister should be. I long for the chaos and clutter, the squabbles and stress I know another child would bring to our lives. I pray they'll come. Soon. But in spite of what's been lost, in spite of what I hope will someday be, there's goodness here. Right now. With you.

—LETTER TO ELLIE, MARCH 7, 2013

Chapter 6

MARCH: JIM AND LAURA

I park my car at the local Friendly's on a Sunday afternoon after church and try to decide what to order. I haven't eaten at a Friendly's since I was a waitress at the one in my hometown for a few summers during high school. I spent long days then scooping ice cream and serving French fries and burgers to tourists. Today, I'm here to talk with Jim and Laura Lavelle, a couple from my church whom I hardly know.

I first met Laura about four months ago at a women's ministry function called Table Talks, where women of all ages were invited to eat breakfast together, get to know one another, and share experiences of God's faithfulness in their lives. *Because everyone has a story*, the advertisement in the church bulletin read.

Everyone does have a story worth telling—I believe that wholeheartedly. But the truth is, I was in no mood to attend on that particular morning. Just weeks away from Avaleen's anticipated due date, I was feeling her absence profoundly. Even though I knew I'd experienced God's faithfulness in the past, my grief was so thick I could barely think of anything else to talk about, let alone recount an inspiring tale of God's work in my life. Plus, I knew there would be assigned seating, designed to help us meet other women outside of our familiar circles. As an introvert who finds it difficult to engage new people on my best days, this made the event even less appealing.

"I don't want to go," I whined to CJ. "I don't have anything to say, especially to a bunch of people I don't know."

"You don't have to go," he replied, patient.

But I did end up going. Even a morning of forced conversation with strangers sounded slightly better, or at least slightly more original, than sitting at home with my sadness—again.

At my assigned table, I did my best to carry my end of the conversation with those around me: a young single professional, a few older married women, and a college student, most of whom I'd never met. I listened as several shared their stories about how God met them in severe illness and during parenting difficulties, and then, knowing I had to leave a bit early to make it to another event on time, I blurted out the only thing I could think to share: my story. All of it spilled out through my tears—the infertility, the miscarriage, the deep anguish I couldn't see beyond. "I know God is faithful," I sniffled apologetically, "but I guess I'm having trouble seeing that right now."

"Oh, honey," one rosy-cheeked grandmother told me gently. "We all feel like that sometimes."

The petite blonde woman beside her reached across the table and handed me a business card that identified her as a graphic designer. "I know you have to go soon," she said, "but sometime I'd like to tell you my story."

———

Still grieving Avaleen, still unable to get pregnant again, I follow up on her invitation and meet Laura and her husband Jim at Friendly's. I'd offered to take them out to lunch, and they'd chosen this spot in part because they'd first developed their friendship here, gathering regularly with other single friends from church after Saturday morning prayer meetings.

We meet in the lobby and then settle into a booth. Laura pulls a pair of large, round reading glasses out of her bag and perches them on her nose, accentuating her pixie cut and delicate features. I watch as she and Jim study their menus. Everything about Laura seems dainty, a marked contrast to Jim's strong, loud presence.

We order, and while we wait for our food to arrive, the Lavelles tell me more about how their friendship began. Jim had become a Christian in high school, and Laura had experienced a dramatic conversion during her college years. Eventually, their paths led them both to our church, where their mutual interests in prayer and nursing home ministry brought them into frequent contact. During regular visits to the nursing home, Laura says, they often found themselves pairing up and "going to visit people together."

For a long time, though, both insist they were nothing more than friends. Then one day, Jim shares matter-of-factly, he was saying goodbye to Laura on their way out of the nursing home, and God spoke to him in a one-word message: *Tag.*

"The next thing that came to my mind," he explains, "was, *You're it.*"

And just like that, Jim, who never thought he would get married or have a family, decided to pursue a relationship with Laura.

I marvel that one simple, somewhat vague word from God could re-orient the entire course of a man's life, and I note that Jim, whom I've never spoken with before today, is a man of bold and confident faith.

As it turns out, God had been speaking to Laura too, drawing her attention to Jim. One Sunday morning during worship, she was praying about three men she was interested in, including Jim. "And then I felt like the Lord said, *Well, wouldn't you want your good friend?*" she recounts. "And I knew exactly who that was."

Shortly thereafter, Jim asked out Laura. "My expectation was that she would say, 'That's very nice thank you, but I can't do it. I'm becoming a nun. I'm going anywhere away from you.'" He laughs, broad shoulders shaking.

"I said, 'Well I've been praying about it,'" Laura continues, drawing, as she does at several points throughout our interview, on an image to explain her emotions. "'And I see our relationship as a rose bud that's just starting to open up' . . . He was thrilled."

I haven't known them long, but it's obvious that Jim and Laura are an excellent match. They laugh at each other's jokes and listen to one another intently. Later, after we've finished lunch and moved our conversation to the living room of their tiny town home, their compatibility becomes even clearer.

"Jim used to make me laugh," Laura explains. "He still does. We laugh a lot . . . Being around Jim, I lighten up more." She elaborates, "My baby pictures are—" She pauses, looking straight ahead with a serious expression. "His are—" She stops again, twisting her mouth into a grin.

"Never a frown in any of them," Jim finishes for her. "Always a smile."

As they tell it, their relationship progressed quickly, and they were engaged within three months, then married eleven months after that.

Because Jim never thought he would get married, he didn't have a strong desire to be a parent, but he was open to one or two kids. Laura, however, deeply longed for children. "I always wanted to be a mom," she says. "Since I was a little girl, I loved playing with dolls."

The Lavelle's dog, Angel, a small, white terrier, jumps up on the couch next to where I'm sitting and snuggles beside me. I pat her head, thinking of how I too always knew I wanted to be a mother.

At the time, Laura was working as a secretary in the church office, and Jim was an associate at Marshalls. They felt there was no way they could afford a child. But a few months into marriage, Jim was able to get a better job with a realty company, and they decided to begin trying to grow their family. Jim was forty; Laura was thirty-six. They got pregnant immediately.

"I was so happy," Laura says. "I was so excited . . . [God] gave me the desire of my heart."

"It was exciting," Jim adds. "And scary. Gotta grow up now."

Unable to contain her joy, Laura immediately told everyone the news. Because of her age, her pregnancy was considered high-risk, so her doctor's office scheduled her for an ultrasound at eight weeks. "When they did the ultrasound," Laura explains, "they were having trouble. And then they said . . . there was no heartbeat, but they could see there had been a baby that was measuring probably about six weeks."

The nurse practitioner at the office explained to Jim and Laura what would happen when her body actually began to miscarry and then sent them to the hospital for a second ultrasound to confirm the loss.

Laura's voice breaks. "It was a really hard day."

For Jim, the ultrasound was especially challenging. "It seemed like it was very cold," he says, referring to both the atmosphere of the place and the demeanor of the technician. "I remember the technician doing the ultrasound [was] sort of like, 'Well, the doctor will be right in.'"

He continues, "It was kind of hard. Well, not kind of hard; it was hard. I remember thinking, *How do you mourn someone you haven't met before?*"

For Laura, one of the comforts of that day was a song she believes God put in her heart: "Jesus, Lover of My Soul." I know the song well, though it's been years since I've heard it. Laura highlights several lines that were significant for her: *It's all about You, Jesus . . . It's not about me as if You should do things my way. You alone are God and I surrender to Your ways.*[8]

"Somehow," she says, "I knew it was about Him, and I needed to surrender to Him."

---

8. Oakley, "Jesus, Lover of My Soul," lines 1-7.

It would be another three weeks before Laura's body began to show signs of miscarrying. "I was starting to recover and get back into the swing of things," Laura says. "Then the miscarriage actually happened. I had a lot of cramping," she recalls. "It was bad."

Jim and Laura named their baby Alpha after one of the lines in the "Jesus, Lover of My Soul" song: *Alpha and Omega, you have loved me.*[9]

"It seemed like the perfect name to both of us," Laura says.

The days following the miscarriage were particularly difficult for both Jim and Laura. "I just did a lot of listening," Jim says.

"We cried a lot together," Laura continues.

"[My] shoulders got bigger."

They took some time and drove west to Shenandoah, traveling Skyline Drive. They talked to friends who'd experienced miscarriage and stillbirth. Still, Laura struggled deeply. At one point, she remembers telling her mom, "I just don't want to live anymore."

She did, however, find hope in the thought of another child. "I think we assumed we'd get pregnant again," Laura says.

But when the Lavelles started trying again, months and months went by with no pregnancy. "Every month, every kind of symptom," Laura says, "and you think, *Oh, this is it!* I tell you it ruins your whole day when your period starts. Months, years of that, it's horrible. It's horrible."

I nod, knowing what she means. My own experience of infertility only lasted for one terrible year, and I can imagine how Laura's pain must have deepened as time passed.

Jim felt the emotional upheaval too. "It's like every month, *Okay, maybe this time now, maybe this is it.* And then it's not."

Eventually, they decided to pursue testing to determine the cause of their infertility, but the results were unhelpful. "Nothing was wrong," Laura says.

Here too, Laura wrestled deeply. "I would give my disappointments to Him all the time. Every month. *Why? I don't understand.* I don't think I was angry or anything like that; it was just disappointment."

"I didn't think it was anything God was doing to me," Jim agrees. "God works in everything; there's His plan."

Eventually, after a little over three years of marriage and more than two years of infertility, they decided to pursue adoption, opting for a path they believed offered a higher probability of a baby than IVF. They attended

9. Ibid., lines 14-15.

classes at the adoption agency they'd chosen and put together several copies of an album for birth parents to browse. They set up a nursery in their home and bought a car seat and stroller. Laura crocheted a blanket for their baby and even spent time researching how to introduce an infant to their dog. "We did a lot of preparation and reading," she says.

At the same time, the two of them also volunteered in the one-year-olds' class at our church. Laura had been involved with the class for some time, but a friend, knowing they were interested in adoption, suggested that Jim also sign up to get some experience relating to small children. According to Laura, Jim was a big hit with the one-year-old crowd. "The kids loved him," she says.

During the months they waited with their names on the list at the adoption agency, Laura was laid off from the church office. She didn't immediately pursue a new job, in part because she was planning to stay home full-time when the baby arrived. At the same time, Jim also had a career change. Feeling the need to move on from his realty job, he accepted a lower-paying position at Walmart.

When the phone call finally came telling them a baby was waiting, Jim and Laura had to tell the agency that their financial situation had changed. The agency asked for a report, which Laura sent.

Later that day, another call came from the agency. Laura was out, so Jim answered. A verdict had been reached: "Not on the list anymore," Jim says.

While both Jim and Laura were deeply disappointed, Laura found this situation easier to accept than her miscarriage. "I still kept hoping we'd have a baby of our own."

At first, she and Jim planned to continue pursuing an adoption once Jim's job situation improved, and when he finally did get a better job eight or nine months later, they called and asked to be put back on the list. But just one month later, they were no longer certain and requested to be removed. "The desire wasn't there anymore," Laura says. "We just felt like God was saying no."

Even now, they don't understand why God led them down the road of adoption and then closed the door. "It doesn't make sense that He would say yes and then He would say no," Laura muses. "I don't know. I guess He needed to bring us through something."

I don't understand either. It seems so unfair.

While Laura felt peace about not adopting, she continued to mourn the biological child she miscarried. "I was still grieving the loss of our baby because even if you adopted, it wouldn't be a Jim and Laura." She takes a sip of water, and the ice clinks against her glass.

It's been almost a decade since the adoption fell through, Laura explains. For many of those years, she and Jim continued to hope for a pregnancy, even as each year their odds of conceiving dropped dramatically.

It wasn't an easy time. In addition to the continued monthly disappointment, there was growing fear about the fact that they might never have children. Laura recalls crying and asking for prayer at a church meeting, only to be told by a friend, "Well, maybe you're not going to have kids." Though this friend turned out to be right, her words were hurtful at the time.

Only in the past few years, as first Jim and then Laura have entered their fifties, have they come to peace with not having children. For Jim, the moment happened a few years ago, and in keeping with his matter-of-fact personality, it was simple and direct and free from emotional turmoil. "It was like, 'Okay, I don't think it's going to happen,'" he recalls. "What next? Got nieces and nephews and babies in care group that I can look at."

For Laura, who just turned fifty recently, the process was more gradual. "It's like through the years, the desire lessened, and now it's really not much of a desire," she explains.

These days, she's busy starting her own graphic design business and loving on Angel. She and Jim seem happy and fulfilled, absent of bitterness, and content with life as it is. I want to know how that can be, how it's possible to continue trusting in the God who has withheld one of your deepest longings.

"How do you see God in the story of your life?" I ask, fumbling for the right words.

Jim references Ps 16:6, which reads: *The lines have fallen for me in pleasant places; indeed, I have a beautiful inheritance.* He explains its significance: "What the tapestry's going to look like on the other side of eternity? I don't know, but I know God's always done good even through the worst of things. I've never had any doubt of that."

I envy Jim's certain faith. I believe what he's saying, that he's never really doubted God's goodness. He reminds me of CJ, who—in spite of very real feelings of sorrow and disappointment—has always been able to somehow see God's faithfulness above and apart from these emotions.

"It actually is a choice you make to rejoice," Jim continues. He's right about our inability to change our circumstances, about our need to choose joy in them. And yet, I feel conflicted as I listen to him. I've never been the kind of person who's found it easy to trust God in difficult circumstances; I've always needed to wrestle through the pain and the questions to find peace. I don't know how to relate to God any other way.

There are many different ways to grieve, to respond to God in the midst of a challenging situation. And God can handle all of it: those of us who struggle deeply, those of us who, for whatever reason, don't have to.

"God is there," Jim says. "And God has always been there. I never felt alone."

God met Jim, and God also met Laura, even in her many years of disappointment. "He loves us," she says simply. "He loves our souls."

I'm reminded of the song God gave her the day of her miscarriage, "Jesus, Lover of My Soul." Somehow, all of the hardship Laura has walked through with God has helped her see His love for her more clearly. Part of me wants to hear something deeper, something more striking or profound, but perhaps, I realize, this is sometimes all there is: God's sustaining presence and comfort in our pain, even the pain we cannot understand.

While their childlessness remains largely a mystery to them, the Lavelles do see God's hand in some of their circumstances, particularly in leading Laura to a job as a graphic designer at a crisis pregnancy center called Sanctity of Life Ministries, a job she wouldn't have taken if she'd had children at home. At first, Laura didn't want to be there because it was difficult to be around women who wanted to end their pregnancies when she wanted more than anything to be pregnant again. However, eventually, Laura says, "I saw that I was called to be there for . . . that time."

Jim finds comfort in the fact that God used Laura in her job, perhaps to help save a baby's life. He imagines one of the ads she's created bringing an abortion-minded woman to the pregnancy center and, in the end, leading her to choose life. "You don't know what you've done," he says to Laura.

"That's true," she muses.

Both Jim and Laura speak too of how they've been able to better care for those around them who have suffered similar losses. "It makes your prayers more passionate, more real," Laura says.

But she admits she often doesn't know what to say to someone suffering from infertility or miscarriage. "When you want children so badly that you cry every month when you're not pregnant," she says, "how can somebody's testimony that . . . God had different plans for us, how can that encourage anybody? I don't know."

"I know what you're saying," I respond. "Of course when you're in the middle of wanting to have more children, there's part of you that wants to feel that everyone gets to do that, but at the same time you also know that's not the case."

I think of what Brian said last month about how testimonies with happy endings can be challenging when you're not sure how your own story will turn out. And I think that those of us struggling to have children desperately need to hear from people like Laura. We need to hear that God can meet us and care for us even if our worst fears of not having children come true. I want to tell Laura that her story matters, that it does encourage me, but before I get the chance, she turns the conversation toward me.

"You have a wonderful little girl," she tells me. "And if that's all God blesses you with, you're going to have a great relationship with her. You three, you know, that's a nice number. And you'll be a really close family."

I nod, suddenly and deeply aware of the precious gift I've been given in Ellie. I see her through Laura's eyes, from the vantage point of a woman who never got to hold the child she longed for. I am convicted of my own discontent, but mostly I feel the heart of Laura's words: a call to find joy and see God in my present reality, just as she and Jim have worked so hard to do in year after year of disappointment.

———

I come back often to Laura's words in the days that follow as I prepare for Ellie's upcoming second birthday party.

I cut out Curious George water-bottle labels and cupcake toppers, and I think about my sweet daughter and the precious days we get to spend together—full of mud-puddle stomping and Play-Doh and muffin baking and lots and lots of snuggly book reading. And for the first time I allow myself to imagine life with Ellie as our only child to be a good thing, a wonderful thing even. I've always thought having one child would be sad and lonely, but the truth is our family right now doesn't feel sad or lonely at all. There's life and laughter, and I realize Laura's right. Three *is* a nice number, and if that's all we're given, there is and will be joy here.

Less than two weeks later, we find out that I am pregnant again.

I found out this morning what I'd been suspecting for almost a week: I'm pregnant again. I'd actually put off testing the past few days for reasons I can't fully explain. I think I just wasn't ready to take on the emotional weight of what it means to be pregnant. There's a lot to it, and now that I know for sure, some of the layers are starting to sink in.

—JOURNAL ENTRY, MARCH 28, 2013

Chapter 7

APRIL: JARED AND KIM

I know I should feel excited and grateful, and on some level, I do. But most of all, I feel numb. The test says there's a baby growing inside me, but all I can think about is how it will feel if we lose this one too.

I calculate in my head and realize this baby will be due in November, almost exactly a year after Avaleen should have been born. One year ago, just before Ellie's first birthday, I'd learned I was pregnant for the second time. Now, days before her second birthday, I'm pregnant again. It feels strange, and I can't help but wonder if this year will be a repeat of the last.

So Ellie will be a little older than two and a half when this baby is born, I think. Or rather, I correct myself, *if this baby is born.*

Days later, over Easter morning breakfast with my parents and Joel and Jen, CJ and I tell them our news. They're excited for us, but I feel uncomfortable—in part because of their attention, in part because of the uncertainty. "I don't know how to engage my heart," I admit. "I can't believe we're actually going to have a baby."

Because of my history of miscarriage, my obstetrician wants to see me early—at six weeks. The day of the appointment, the waves of nausea I've started to feel have faded. Frantic, I pull spices out of my pantry cabinet, sniffing cumin and chili powder and garlic, willing my stomach to turn. Nothing. I convince myself that this baby is already gone.

But at my appointment, in the same room where I first saw Avaleen's stillness, we make out the tiniest flicker of a heartbeat. I feel relived but not relaxed, even when the nausea hits me with full force a few days later. We lost Avaleen at fourteen and a half weeks, and until we are well past that point in this pregnancy, I'll wonder if the same unknown thing that took her from me will take this baby too.

I feel awful, just as I have in my two previous pregnancies. In a strange way, though, the consuming nature of my sickness is helpful. I'm so busy trying to take care of Ellie and keep my own food in my stomach that I don't have the luxury of time to reflect and become anxious. Every day, I wonder if the baby is still doing okay, if we'll see its heartbeat at my next doctor's appointment, but I don't have time to get stuck there. I'm too busy just getting by.

My interview this month is with old friends from college, Jared and Kim Erb, who live out of town. I spend the week leading up to our meeting wondering whether or not to tell them I'm pregnant. CJ and I haven't shared the news widely, and I worry that a pregnancy announcement will make my own story the focus of our time together. I decide to keep quiet and pack my purse full of the peppermint gum and carb-laden snacks to help keep my nausea at bay.

I've arranged to meet Jared and Kim at their home in a suburb of Lancaster, Pennsylvania, a short drive from my parents' house in the city. It's been a few years since I've seen them and almost fifteen since we first met. Jared was a senior when I'd joined the Navigators campus ministry as a freshman, so I interacted with him only from a distance. I knew Kim more closely, having lived directly across the dorm hall from her my junior year. We stayed in touch through weddings and baby showers for mutual friends and at the occasional reunion, but we never got into the habit of talking regularly after college.

I'm looking forward to seeing them again. Kim is a woman characterized by joy, someone who is quick to laugh and puts people at ease. And Jared, a skateboarding enthusiast and special education teacher turned principal, has always impressed me with his laid-back confidence. I don't know their four children, but I'm excited to meet them.

It's a sunny Saturday afternoon when I pull up to the Erbs's house, accompanied by Ellie. I spot Jared pushing a lawn mower, and it seems there are children everywhere: streaks of motion on scooters, bikes, and running feet. Jared turns off the mower to say hello and introduces a clingy

Ellie and me to his two oldest boys, Colson and Davison. The pair stops running around with the neighbor kids long enough to greet me and show off a new baseball bat acquired at a yard sale earlier that day. Minutes later, Kim meets me at the front door with a warm hello and an introduction to her daughter, Kyla, who—just a few months older than Ellie—is eager to show us her bedroom.

I sit with Kim on the floor in Kyla's room while she and Ellie play, and we chat about the yard sale and their new next-door neighbors—a family with seven kids—many of whom were part of the swarm I spotted when we first pulled up. The baby, Jayden, wakes from his nap full of smiles. Kim and I take him and the girls downstairs to baby dolls, dinner preparation, and, eventually, the backyard swing set.

I split my time between playing with Ellie and Kyla and talking with Kim when she isn't busy cooking, feeding the baby, or periodically checking in on the boys' outdoor adventures. When dinner is ready, we gather the kids around a wooden picnic table and sit down to plates of grilled chicken and vegetables, macaroni and cheese, and fresh bread. Mercifully, the food doesn't make me nauseous, and amidst spills and portion-control guidance and vegetable-eating interventions, we manage a few snippets of adult conversation.

It's well after eight by the time everyone is settled. The big kids are in bed, my parents have come to pick up Ellie for a sleepover, and Jayden rocks in a swing near us—the muted hum of the motor steady in the background. I know Jared and Kim are tired from their long day, but they brew coffee and settle onto the couch with a bag of pistachio nuts between them, ready to jump into their story.

"I have a recording of myself when I was three or four saying that I loved Jesus," Jared begins.

"Do you?" Kim asks, looking up from her pistachios to stare at him. "I didn't know that."

Jared goes on to describe growing up in a Christian home, his mother Charismatic, his father more conservative. Because his parents had difficulty agreeing on a church, Jared spent much of his childhood hopping from congregation to congregation. It was at a Christian Missionary Alliance church in sixth grade where he made a commitment to follow Christ.

Before Jared can tell us any more, we hear tentative footsteps coming down the steps. A wide pair of eyes peek into the living room soon after. "Daddy, we're looking at the Bible," Davison announces.

"That's wonderful," Kim says warmly. I smile. I know that even the sweetest of interruptions can turn into drawn-out bedtime battles, but I can't help enjoying this one.

"That's fine," Jared says with a touch of firmness. "But don't interrupt us, because we're in a really big conversation. Okay?"

"You guys can read the Bible and then go to bed," Kim instructs.

"Come get us if you need us," Jared says, watching as Davison begins to climb the stairs before returning to his story. "Sixth grade I stepped forward in faith. Seventh grade I stepped backward into the party scene."

Jared summarizes the next three years as full of worldly pursuits. "God allowed me to be very, very humbled," he says. Desperate for another way, Jared began to study the Bible. "I plunged into Scripture," he says. It "wasn't just words on a page; God was speaking to me in the Word and basically reforming my soul."

He references Matt 11:28: *Come to me, all who labor and are heavy laden, and I will give you rest.* "I had this huge burden from all this sin," he explains. "I remember a sense of God taking that burden and a sense of peace replacing it."

Kim also grew up in a Christian home, but her own journey with God was less tumultuous. "This probably sounds silly to say, but I just feel like I loved Jesus growing up."

It doesn't sound silly to me; I felt the same way as a child, dancing during worship in the back of the fire hall our congregation rented each Sunday. While Kim admits she may have had small doubts in high school or focused too much on being popular, she never wavered in her desire to live for God. This is my story too.

Both she and Jared attribute much of their spiritual growth to their college years with the Navigators. Because Jared is four years older than Kim, they were never actually students together in the campus ministry, but their paths crossed anyway, at the wedding of a Navigator couple they both knew.

Jared remembers seeing Kim for the first time, "I turned around and . . . I saw her smile. And it was just like, *Wow, there's some serious joy in this person.*"

Kim was immediately attracted to Jared as well, especially when she discovered how much they had in common: both grew up in Lancaster, both attended Penn State, both trained as teachers. But the day after meeting at the wedding, Kim was leaving for a mission trip to Thailand for about six weeks, and shortly after she returned, Jared was heading back to his teaching job in Massachusetts. They only had a short window of time to get to know each other.

On their first date, they went out for ice cream and ended up running into a bunch of Navigator friends. "Were you part of our first date?" Kim asks. "A lot of people were."

It takes me a few moments, but eventually I'm able to remember the scene: picnic benches in a parking lot on a dark summer night, ice cream cones and laughter, and the slight awkwardness of a new couple running into a bunch of single friends.

Their second date, Jared says, was a week at the ocean with his family.

"I went Wednesday to Sunday," Kim clarifies. "We had some connections. On our first date, my mom realized his sister and my cousin were best friends . . . it wasn't like I was just going to the beach with a strange guy."

After their vacation, Jared returned to New England and Kim began her senior year at Penn State. Their long-distance relationship progressed quickly, and a little over a year after they met, they were married.

Kim joined Jared in Massachusetts, where he was teaching life skills at a middle school, and she took a job teaching high school math. They didn't worry too much about having children at first.

"We both knew we wanted a family," Kim says. "We were never specific. In general, we probably thought maybe three."

"In all honesty," Jared adds. "I was just happy to be married."

Between adjusting to jobs and marriage and eventually to a move back to Lancaster, it was about four years before the Erbs felt ready to start trying. Within a few months, they were pregnant.

But at seven weeks, Kim began to spot, and a visit to the obstetrician revealed there was no heartbeat. A miscarriage was beginning. The Erbs grieved the loss of their baby, but they weren't stuck in a place of mourning for long. "It was sad," Kim says, "but we were able to move on . . . I'd heard of a lot of people who had one [miscarriage] . . . and then had a kid."

Their hope for a baby increased at a Bible study one night shortly after the miscarriage, when a man the Erbs had never met before asked if he could pray over them. Kim and Jared agreed, and this man prophesied several things about their lives and mission as a couple. He also said he pictured Kim holding a child. That night, Kim says, she "felt so clearly we were going to have a baby in October. I even told our families we were going to have a baby in October. We weren't pregnant yet."

One of her siblings expressed concern, telling her, "Whoa, Kim! Guard your heart!"

But Kim was, in fact, soon pregnant again, due in early October. Because of her previous miscarriage, the doctor ordered extra tests and put Kim on progesterone supplements. "I was concerned," Kim says. "You get to the point of seven weeks, and it's like, is this going to happen again?"

I've asked myself the same question countless times these past few weeks. I'm eight weeks pregnant now, still six and a half weeks away from the point when we lost Avaleen. I'm anxious about miscarrying this baby now, but I'll feel even more terrified then.

Jared recalls how they prayed for the baby throughout Kim's pregnancy, "Lord, we just have open hands with this. We feel like You've blessed us this far . . . and we love you either way, but we really, with open hands, we want to ask for this child."

God did answer their prayers, and Colson Elijah was born on October 1 via a scheduled C-section. The Erbs were delighted with their son and with their new role as parents. Because of the miscarriage they'd experienced prior to Colson's birth, Jared says, they were very aware that "life is so precious and tender and vulnerable." They prayed every single night for their son's safety.

By the time Colson was about nine or ten months old, they felt they were ready to open the door to the possibility of more children. Before his first birthday, Kim learned she was pregnant again. However, just a day or two later, she started bleeding and miscarried. Because this happened so quickly, before they'd even had the chance to tell anyone, "there wasn't much emotion," Kim says.

Within several months, the Erbs learned that Kim was pregnant once more. But a week later, while visiting family in Baltimore, she began to bleed. "I freaked out," she says. "Called my doctor to get progesterone. I thought that was the issue. He gave me some; it didn't help." She pauses briefly, then continues, "That one was hard."

Still, the Erbs were convinced they'd have more children. Once again, it was only a few months before Kim was pregnant. "I really thought this time something was for real," she says. "I thought, *Okay, Lord, can this really happen again?* I mean we just had two miscarriages."

The doctor put her on progesterone right away and monitored her hormone levels via weekly blood draws. Everything seemed fine. But at around six weeks, Kim felt a weird shooting pain in her shoulder. "I read online it could be ectopic," she says. But she wasn't sure. "*Wouldn't I be bleeding?*" she remembers thinking. The pain worsened, becoming so intense that she called her doctor's office. They told her, "Oh you've had so many [miscarriages]. It's probably just another one. Wait it out."

Finally, though, she couldn't stand it anymore. "I don't remember if it was me or you," Jared says, "but one of us made the statement, 'You know what? We're going in.'"

They drove to the emergency room.

"I can't even describe the pain," Kim says.

At the ER, the technicians came out to perform an ultrasound. "They're kind of relaxed," Kim says. "And all of the sudden the doctor's in there, and it's like, 'We're taking you back to surgery.'"

"They got serious very quickly," Jared continues.

The Erbs learned that the embryo had implanted itself in Kim's right Fallopian tube, which had ruptured as a result, causing excessive internal bleeding. "If I'd waited the night out at home," Kim says, "I could have died. Really I probably would've."

Doctors performed surgery and removed the affected Fallopian tube. The Erbs were thankful for Kim's safety, but they worried that the absence of one of her tubes would make having another child even more difficult. This fourth miscarriage marked the beginning of a period of significant struggle, a season Kim refers to as her "bondage years."

She clarifies her use of that term, "I was in bondage in terms of [being] enslaved, like I *have* to have another child."

At this point, she and Jared underwent testing to see if they could discover any underlying causes of their miscarriages. "Not that there's anything wrong with [the testing]," Kim says, "but I felt like for me it almost consumed me. It did consume me. I wanted a reason; I wanted to know why."

I can relate. I've felt that same consuming desire to understand, to have a reason. I still feel it from time to time. I think about Kim's use of the word "bondage" and wonder if I too have been held captive by my search for answers. I remember Mark's comment about how Job had to repent of his quest to understand, and again, my conscience is pricked. *What does it look like to trust? How can I ask real questions and seek real answers without being consumed by them?*

For the Erbs, testing was inconclusive. The only possibility the specialist could offer was that Kim's C-section scar had not healed well, which possibly caused implantation difficulties. Other than redoing her C-section procedure to see if they could help the scar heal better, there were no answers or possible treatments. The Erbs weren't excited about Kim enduring the risks of another C-section, especially with one missing Fallopian tube already making pregnancy less likely. They decided to keep trying and see what would happen. This time, months passed without a pregnancy.

During this period of testing and waiting, both Jared and Kim grappled with questions about whether or not the miscarriages were a sign that God was judging them. "We went and had people pray for us and prophesy," Jared says. "And everybody saw us with a big family and many kids . . . and so we were like, 'Whoa, is it our lack of faith?'"

"Your mind is so consumed," Kim explains. "You kind of wrestle down every road of why? *Why?*"

Though they continued to be grateful for Colson, the Erbs hated that they couldn't give him a sibling. "It would have been the perfect timing to have another child," Jared says. "You feel like the space is getting away from us, or everybody else is having their next and their next."

I nod, knowing exactly what he means.

Nearing two, Colson—who loved babies—began talking regularly about Chatters and Jeeters. Jared and Kim couldn't figure out who he was referring to until one day Kim finally asked him directly. "He said, 'Mom, they're my brothers.' We said, 'What do you mean your brothers?' He said, 'Remember, they're with Jesus.'" Kim found comfort in his words, as they reminded her that even though she'd miscarried early in her pregnancies, her babies were real children, now in heaven with Jesus.

But she watched with longing as her sister, two sisters-in-law, and numerous friends announced pregnancies and birthed babies. "During those six months of trying, I could literally name fifteen people that were pregnant," she says. And these weren't acquaintances, Kim clarifies, but people with whom she interacted regularly.

I do the math and realize I was probably one of those fifteen people. My heart is heavy as I recall Kim attending my baby shower, graciously participating in games, and watching me open presents for Ellie. I think too about the baby now growing inside me and feel the uncomfortable weight of my own blessings. I know the heartache of one miscarriage, the difficulty of waiting for a pregnancy, but to keep losing babies—this seems too much for anyone to endure.

Jared's words interrupt my thoughts. "It was all you could think about," he says to Kim gently.

Kim turns to me. "And he got annoyed at that because it was hard for him, but then he was ready to move on."

Jared opens his mouth to protest, but Kim continues, "That's okay to say; it's true."

Jared explains, "The tough thing is for me, I was just happy . . . I'm happy to be alive myself. I'm happy to have a wife who loves me, and I [think], *Wow, we have a house . . . I'm thankful to have a son.*"

"And he would take it as I was ungrateful versus this is just a struggle," Kim clarifies.

"She often felt like I wasn't connecting with her pain to the level that I should be, nor was I showing enough sympathy even though I would try," Jared says. "But I couldn't."

I can relate to this too, as CJ and I have experienced a similar dynamic. He grieved Avaleen deeply and openly, but he didn't feel isolated or jealous of others as a result. I wanted his emotions to mirror my own and would became angry when they didn't. I felt like he couldn't understand me, and I was desperate to be understood.

In the midst of this time for the Erbs, a few weeks before Christmas, Kim began to experience excruciating stomach pain. She'd just had her period, so she assumed it wasn't pregnancy-related. Thinking it might be her appendix, she and Jared visited their family doctor, who ordered a pregnancy test. It was positive. They went to the hospital immediately, where doctors ordered an ultrasound. "They at first told us there was a cyst on the ovary," Kim says. "And there's no baby in the uterus at all, not even a sac."

It was a Friday night, so they had to wait with this news for an hour or two before a specialist arrived. When one finally did show up, he told Kim he was going to have to remove her other Fallopian tube. "I lost it," she says, "because I thought he was telling me we would never have kids."

Kim was whisked into surgery immediately, and Jared was left alone. He knew the procedure was supposed to last an hour, but time passed with no word from the doctors. One and a half hours. Two hours. Two and a half hours.

"I thought I was losing her," Jared says. "I seriously thought my wife was dying."

When the doctors finally emerged from surgery, they told Jared the delay had been caused by a computer system malfunction mid-surgery.

They also informed Kim and Jared that the pregnancy had formed outside of the uterine wall, growing from Kim's ovaries toward her uterus. "The doctor said this was the weirdest thing they'd ever seen," Jared recounts.

Fortunately, there hadn't been a need to remove Kim's second tube after all, but there was no guarantee that the ovary itself wasn't damaged. For the Erbs, this second ectopic pregnancy marked a significant turn in their journey.

"From that point," Jared says, "it was just like, wow, this is dangerous."

"I was sad we weren't having a baby," Kim adds. "I was thankful I was alive."

Jared and Kim began to seriously consider adoption. Kim was reading through the Bible at the time and remembers "being impressed with God's calling us to take care of the needy and the poor." She also read several books, including Francis Chan's evangelical best-seller, *Crazy Love*, in which Chan talks about giving up our material and physical comforts for the sake of the poor. "I was starting to get this," Kim says. "This is really hard and this is really sad, and yet there is so much more to God."

At the same time, she also remembers watching several close family members and friends walking through particularly difficult trials—unrelated to fertility. "In a weird way," she explains, "it gave me some healing in my circumstance because it made me say, everybody has their thing."

"Let's talk about the dirt though," Jared interrupts. "It was hard for you."

"It was hard," Kim agrees.

I appreciate their insistence on honesty, even as they are describing the way God was beginning to heal them. In my own experience, I've learned that seeing God in loss doesn't necessarily equal a lessening of pain.

"If people said too much," Jared says, "it was easy for you to get offended. If people didn't say enough, it was easy for you to get offended . . . I remember hearing you so many nights just processing your heart of, 'I don't want to be the weird one. I don't want to be the one that people have pity on.'"

Kim explains that she found it challenging when friends would be extra sensitive in sharing their pregnancy news with her. "Although I appreciated that," she says, "it was like, again, I'm the weird one." She continues, "I started to feel like the woman in the Bible because after all that had happened, I literally bled almost all the time . . . and every time we would have faith to get healing or believe, it's like a worse situation would come."

Kim drew comfort from Scriptures like Ps 126: 1–2a: *When the Lord restored the fortunes of Zion . . . our mouth was filled with laughter, and our tongue with shouts of joy.*

"I felt like God kept giving me this promise that someday there will be joy again in this," Kim says.

Then Jared made a career switch from teaching to administration, and they moved into their current home, significantly increasing their available space. "Our vision," Jared explains, "was that we would be a family and this would be a house of light . . . As we were praying about it, I was just like, 'Let's fill it. Let's fill the house.'"

The more they prayed and thought about it, the more the Erbs were drawn to pursuing adoption through the foster care system. While they were open to both domestic and international adoptions, they didn't want to wait the two or more years those routes would likely take. In addition, Kim says, "God changed our hearts beyond just having a kid to taking care of a child."

I'm struck by her words, by this significant shift in her and Jared's thinking. Through profound suffering, the Erbs's desire to grow their family moved beyond fulfillment of their own dreams and developed into a longing to love and bless others. I hear Jesus in her words, echoes of His selfless love, and I think of how much my own quest for children has been wrapped up in me, of how little it has been about Him.

This isn't to say that fostering was an easy decision for Jared and Kim. They feared loving children who might eventually be returned to biological parents, and they admit that others close to them shared these fears as well. Kim recalls a friend who pulled aside Jared and said, "Your wife has been through so much disappointment and pain; you can't take your family through that pain again."

I don't know if I would have had the courage to say something similar, but I understand their friend's response. Becoming foster parents seems particularly tenuous and risky, especially for people who have already experienced so much suffering. "Did you struggle at all with how pursuing foster care would impact Colson?" I ask, voicing one of my own greatest concerns about adoption.

"Oh, yeah!" Jared says. "We even had family members say, 'We just feel so bad for Colson. What all of this is going to make him give up.' He was the all-star. He was the mascot. Everywhere we went, it was all about him."

Jared goes on to explain that while they knew there were risks for their son related to the foster experience, given Colson's personality and temperament, there were also risks in allowing him to remain an only child.

This insight resonates deeply. I think about our fear-driven culture, about the lengths to which we'll go in hopes of avoiding hurt. I don't want or like pain any more than anyone else, and I spend a fair amount of energy seeking to escape it. But I've never considered Jared's point before, the idea that running from risk is a risk in and of itself, that in trying so hard to protect ourselves from pain, we're also protecting ourselves from opportunities, growth, and joy.

The Erbs welcomed their first foster child, a baby boy, into their family shortly after Colson's third birthday. "My stomach was all the way down to my feet when we took that step of faith," Jared says.

While Jared and Kim quickly grew to love their new son, the foster system placed him with relatives after just four months. Davison arrived a month later, and then, unexpectedly, their first foster son was returned to their home. Suddenly, Jared and Kim were parents to three boys under four.

In the end, their first foster son was reunited with his birth mother after an extended stay with the Erbs, this one lasting almost a full year. While it was difficult to give up a child who'd been part of their home for so long, the Erbs say the process helped them see foster care as an opportunity not only to bless children, but also to serve the adults connected to them. "It opened our eyes up to the mom," Jared says. "We actually became the cheerleaders for her and their whole family."

The Erbs continued fostering Davison, whose adoption should be finalized in the next few months, and then welcomed Kyla and Jayden, Davison's biological brother, into their home. They want to adopt these two children as well, but their futures remain unclear. For now, Jared says, "Our house is full."

"It's plenty full," Kim laughs.

Both Jared and Kim believe that becoming foster parents has helped heal them and allowed them to see redemption in their many losses and disappointments. "We were able to move away from the burden of it," Jared says. Foster care is "an alternative fulfillment" of their longing for more children.

"I realized how you love other children like your own," Kim says. "I mean really. They're not adopted yet, so . . . we have to love with guarded hearts. But there's no doubt in our minds that we love them like our own, 100 percent. 100 percent."

"They're our kids," Jared agrees. "Even though we know they might not be our kids forever, they're our kids for now."

And Colson? "What he gave up," Jared says, "turned into the biggest blessing because it challenged him in such a way that life wasn't all about him anymore."

Both Jared and Kim acknowledge an adjustment period for Colson. In fact, they share, there have been multiple adjustment periods over the past three years as their family structure has continued to change. "He'd say things to us like, 'If they leave, we'll be normal,'" Kim recalls. "And so I said, 'In God's story . . . normal looks different.' It's really cool though. He's really grasped it. Like the day we found out Davison was going to be adopted . . . Colson and Davison just flew around cheering. They ran over to the neighbors' to tell them." I smile, thinking of the sweet work being done in Colson's little soul, even through the difficulties he's faced as a sibling to fostered children.

Challenges remain, however. Two of the Erbs's four children may be returned to their birth families in the months or years to come. Those who stay carry their own stories of abandonment and hurt. And for Kim and Jared, who eventually decided to leave the door open to another biological child in spite of the risks to Kim's body, there have been more miscarriages, four or five since they decided to become foster parents.

They happen early on, Kim explains, and at this point, they don't have much hope she'll ever be able to carry a pregnancy to term. Yet, she says, they continue to allow pregnancies to occur because "God can do miracles."

I'm surprised to hear this, and my immediate reaction is one of concern. At the same time, part of me admires Kim and Jared's faith. Here, too, they're willing to risk more loss and more disappointment, knowing that God can and does show up in miraculous ways.

The baby stirs, and Kim rises to fill a bottle. She returns with Jayden in her arms and begins to feed him while we continue talking. I ask Kim and Jared what they've learned through their journey, what they feel like God has been doing, even in the horrific and unexplainable pain of repeated miscarriages. They discuss the people God has brought into their lives who they're able to relate to and care for, people they likely wouldn't have connected with otherwise. For Kim, this includes family friends and women from her church group for moms. For Jared, it's meant countless opportunities to reach out to foster children and parents as a school administrator.

The Erbs also talk about how they now see their home and their family as a place for mission. "I look at it as a ministry," Jared says, reaching over to wipe Jayden's chin with a burp cloth. "We're joining children and youth and supporting their cause and God's greater cause of caring for the least of these."

The more I listen to Jared and Kim talk, the more I see just that: the story of great suffering God has used to turn the hearts of one family toward a mission they might not otherwise have considered. I think of my own vision of family and how narrow it seems by contrast. Certainly, I want to raise kids who will be followers of Jesus, but if I'm honest, a big part of my dream is to create a home that's a safe haven for me and my family. I tend to see family as a treasure to horde and protect, not a center for a sometimes risky mission.

It's good for me to realize this as I face my constant fears about losing this pregnancy. In many ways, my life is consumed by thinking about risk, by doing everything I can to minimize loss: no caffeine, no dairy, no strenuous exercise, lots of pills and supplements. Already, I've frequently caught myself longing for the day when I'm checked into the hospital, ready to deliver this baby. It feels like then, seven long months from now, things will finally be safe.

But the Erbs's story reminds me that God is not primarily interested in safety; often, He calls His children to risk and to trust. And then He shows up, not necessarily to remove all pain or disappointment, but to be present, to do good, to advance His kingdom. I can't say this eliminates my worry in the weeks that follow, that I go on to joyfully embrace all the uncertainties of this pregnancy without fear, but it does allow a tiny crack to open in the tight grip anxiety has on my soul, to help me see God in the gift of this pregnancy—in spite of all the risk that remains.

I miss you, Avaleen. I trust what I cannot understand, that somehow goodness triumphs even in your death, that someday we will see how even our pain is part of a beautiful story bigger than either of us. I believe this, but I still miss the delight I know it would've been to watch you grow. I'm so sorry I never got to hold you. One day, I hope. One day.

—BLOG POST, MAY 30, 2013,
ON THE ONE-YEAR ANNIVERSARY OF AVALEEN'S DEATH

Chapter 8

MAY: JUSTIN AND SARA

May is a quiet month. Ellie and I go to her weekly music class and on an occasional playdate, but mostly we stay home, once again reduced to survival. My nausea is just as bad as it's been with my other two pregnancies, and I swear I will never do this again. *What if I go through all this and another baby dies?*

My obstetrician schedules me for ultrasounds every two weeks, and it helps to have regular opportunities to check in and see that the pregnancy is progressing as it should. Still, in the few moments of reflection I can manage, I keep thinking that with Avaleen, there was no sign or warning. *It could happen again at any time.*

I'm keenly aware of what May felt like one year ago, when Avaleen was still alive inside me. Then, I filled out our pool application and went to barbeques, confident we'd be meeting our baby in November. This year, I do the same things, but they're weighted now with the reminder of how tenuous life is, how quickly it can slip away. I still can't allow myself to believe the baby inside me will make it to birth. I still don't really expect to hold a child this November.

On a mid-May Saturday, eleven weeks pregnant, I pack a cooler with a sandwich and crackers and begin the four hour drive to Western Pennsylvania to interview Justin and Sara Brode. I first met Sara nearly four years ago, when we were bridesmaids in the wedding of a mutual friend. I drove her from the ceremony to the reception in my aging Saturn sedan, both of us clad in floor-length orange gowns, and we talked briefly of miscarriage that day. She'd experienced two losses, one before and one after the birth of her first child and was, by then, seven months pregnant. CJ and I were only a few months into trying to get pregnant for the first time. Neither she nor I had any idea what the next few years would hold.

It wasn't until we lost Avaleen that I reconnected with Sara, and we shared the details of our stories and our quests for answers. I started reading Sara's blog, Repro Renegade, in which she candidly shared the ups and downs of her and her husband's fertility journey. Sara found a specialist in New York City, the first person who was able to give her some explanation and a treatment plan for her multiple miscarriages. Seeking similar expert help, CJ and I visited the same specialist a month later after Sara's referral.

I've never been to the Brodes's house before, but much of the drive there is familiar. I head west through Maryland and then north into Central Pennsylvania, tracing the route from Northern Virginia toward my alma mater, Penn State University. In spite of my unsettled stomach and lower back pain, I find myself enjoy the drive and peaceful charms of small-town Pennsylvania, which, even after ten years as a Washingtonian, still feels like home, like exhaling. Just north of Altoona, less than an hour from the place locals call Happy Valley, I turn west again, winding up mountains and along back roads I don't know quite as well, passing towns with names like Munster, Portage, and Nanty Glo, along with an array of taxidermists, gun shops, and tiny bars. It's a bright, clear day, and green is everywhere. I feel suddenly hopeful and alive.

When I pull up to the Brodes's home in a quiet, aging suburb of their small college town, I see Sara right away, pulling weeds from a bed at the bottom of their sloping front lawn. The yard is neat and tidy, fresh with dark mulch and new shrubbery, and I can tell she's been busy all morning. She greets me with a hug and walks me around the house to their backyard, where Justin and their son Asher, age six, are playing catch. Asher's still wearing a pair of mismatched Spiderman pajamas.

After exchanging brief greetings, we make our way inside and upstairs to the room where I'll spend the night. On the way, I'm introduced to three-year-old Abby, a curly towhead playing in the bathroom in her own set of mismatched pajamas, very much awake and not in bed, despite, Sara informs me, this being her designated nap time.

Sara helps me settle my bags in the guest bedroom, pointing out a small dish of peppermints and ginger candy she's left on the nightstand to help with my nausea. We'd talked earlier about how I'd probably need to rest in order to stay up for an interview this evening, so after a few moments of conversation, she leaves me to myself. I snuggle beneath crisp, white sheets, a steady spring breeze flowing through the open windows, and look up at the slanted white ceiling that rises to a peak. The room is spacious and fresh, the sort of room I always wanted as a little girl.

I lie there thinking about the kindness wrapped in Sara's candy dish. A few weeks ago, I'd been anxious to tell her I was pregnant, knowing she and Justin have been trying for a few months under the watchful supervision of the specialist. I know how difficult it can be to rejoice over someone else's pregnancy when you desperately wish to be pregnant yourself, and I was afraid my news would hurt her or push her away. But even though I would have understood if she'd needed to disengage, she did the opposite. She entered in. I drift off to sleep, deeply blessed.

An hour or two later, after I've managed a short nap, I wander downstairs to find Justin and the kids playing out back again. Sara's taking a shower. While Abby roams the yard and Justin tosses a baseball with Asher, Justin and I chat. We met at the wedding too, but I'm not sure I've ever spoken more than a few words to him before today. His calm demeanor puts me at ease, and we talk comfortably about church and college and life in Pennsylvania.

Later, while Sara prepares a dinner of roast chicken, mashed potatoes, and cauliflower, I sit at the dining room table and help Abby squeeze glitter from a tube onto a piece of construction paper. Asher draws superhero pictures and makes me a green paper crown, complete with hand-drawn jewels. I wear it during dinner, much to his amusement.

After bedtime routines, the house quiets, and I settle onto a couch across from Justin and Sara. Sara curls her feet under her, and Justin stretches his lanky legs on the coffee table, relaxed. They begin by telling me about their conversion stories, similar in many ways.

Both grew up with some church experience, but without a clear understanding of who God was or any sense of a personal relationship with Him. At their respective colleges, Indiana University of Pennsylvania for Justin and Salisbury University for Sara, both met friends who took them to church, and gradually, both began to see a relationship with God as central to their lives.

They met after college when Justin's teaching job and Sara's work with a lobbying group led them to the DC area, where they ended up in the same church small group. Justin recalls sitting in a friend's basement the moment he first saw Sara. As he puts it, she "came bee-bopping in there with one of her friends, and I was like, 'Whoa! I'd like to get to know her.'"

Sara was drawn to Justin as a friend. "Whenever I would talk to him," she says, "he just makes you feel at ease."

However, when Justin first asked her out, she wasn't sure. It was after a small group meeting, under the glow of a street light. "I remember standing there," Justin says. "Just standing there . . . I can't remember the exact words she said, but it basically amounted to, 'No, loser.'"

We all laugh. In spite of Sara's initial rejection, their friendship continued, and a few months later they began dating. Within a year, they were married.

Sara, whose parents divorced when she was two and who was an only child until thirteen, always wanted a large family. "I had this number five in my head since I was young," she says.

Justin, who grew up with four siblings, imagined a slightly smaller crew. "I've always had three in mind," he says. "I think around that three to five range is what we talked about."

"But Sara," he adds, "she's never let go of that five."

"Nobody expects to have fertility problems," she says. "You think it always happens to other people. That sounds like that ought to be the story of somebody else, not me."

I nod in agreement. In my teens and early twenties, I pictured an ordered, happy life, rarely stopping to dwell on the possible difficulties that might interrupt my plans. Now, as I age and as I witness family and friends deal with many different varieties of suffering, I find myself frequently thinking about what life would look like if I got cancer or CJ was in a car accident or Ellie took a terrible fall at the playground. I try to pray about these things, to stave off worrying by remembering the words of Matt 6:27: *and which of you by being anxious can add a single hour to his span of life?* Often, though, I engage instead in the sort of self-protective logic Sara is describing. *Cancer won't be my story. It's other people who lose children in tragic accidents.* It's too terrifying to admit the truth—that I have very little control over what my story will be.

For Justin and Sara, it was about a year and a half into marriage, after they'd relocated from Northern Virginia to Pennsylvania and settled into new jobs there, when they decided they were ready to expand their family. In a few months, they were pregnant.

However, at about eight weeks, Sara began to spot and went to the hospital for an emergency sonogram. Doctors told her she had a blighted ovum. "It was just a sac," she says. "They never even saw anything really developing."

All the same, it was a difficult time. "I was a mess," Sara says. In particular, she struggled because she'd begun to imagine her future life as a mom. "Not only is it really sad," she reflects, "but there's that loss of direction. Like what am I going to do now?"

Also, she shares, "I struggled a lot with anger after that miscarriage. I remember feeling wronged that no one from church brought us a meal, even though I knew it wasn't something to which I was entitled. But I was angry that we had just lost a member of our family, and angry that no one seemed to understand how hard it was for me to function at that time."

And then there was the awful, physical reality of the miscarriage itself. Her doctors encouraged her to allow her body to miscarry naturally, promising she wouldn't pass anything larger in size than a quarter. "It's terrible," Sara says. "You're bleeding every day, and every time you go to the bathroom and wipe, it's like death. You're reminded every time: *my baby died, my baby died.*"

At one point, Sara says, "something went into the toilet. I didn't really look at it; I felt something." She continues, "It was a lot bigger than a quarter."

I appreciate her candor. Since I elected for a D&E procedure after Avaleen's death, I've sometimes wondered if it would have been physically and emotionally healthier to allow my body to miscarry on its own. Listening to Sara, though, I feel more certain of my own decision. I remember going to the grocery store on the day before my D&E and how terrible it felt to attempt normal life knowing there was a dead baby inside me. I think of Sara's experience, and I imagine weeks of bleeding and the emotional weight of death literally seeping out of my body.

Plus, Avaleen would have been significantly larger than Sara's first child, probably around the size of a lemon. She would have had a face, a body, miniature fingers and toes. The thought of delivering her delicate body into my bathroom toilet, without the help of any medical professionals, makes me feel sick. I still wish I'd tried to deliver her in a hospital, but I'm surer than ever that I wouldn't have wanted to do it at home alone.

Mercifully, Justin and Sara were able to get pregnant again within a few months. At their ten-week appointment, they remember the joy they felt at seeing a tiny baby on the ultrasound screen. "It's the cutest thing," Sara says. "It was like the happiest thing to see that little peanut in there."

I ask the Brodes if they experienced a lot of anxiety prior to that ultrasound as a result of their earlier miscarriage. They both say they think they felt some, but they can't remember. Too much has happened since then.

"I think at that point," Justin says, "we both just kind of felt like we were going to have babies."

After a healthy, relatively easy pregnancy, their son Asher was born. There was no reason for the Brodes to suspect they would have trouble birthing more children in the future. When Asher was a little over a year old, they decided to try again. "I was really sick with that pregnancy," Sara recalls. "I could barely get off the couch, and I hadn't been that way with Asher at all."

Looking back, she wonders if that was the first sign that something with her body was going terribly wrong. Though I felt just as sick with Ellie as I did with Avaleen, I understand. I've spent hours analyzing every detail I can remember about my previous two pregnancies, trying to think of something that was different the second time, something that might have caused Avaleen's death. As mothers, I think, we're desperate to understand what's happening with our bodies, to exercise whatever measure of control we can to protect our children's lives.

Around fifteen or sixteen weeks into her pregnancy, just as she was finally beginning to feel better, Sara noticed some spotting and went to see her doctor, only to discover that there was no heartbeat. This time, she and Justin elected to have a D&C, which doctors performed immediately.

Sara remembers that loss as a sad one, but she also recalls seeing God's kindness clearly. "I think I actually had a lot harder time than Sara," Justin says. "It wasn't crippling for me, but I remember thinking that I was struggling."

For Sara, who'd finished reading the book of Ruth just prior to the miscarriage, there was much encouragement in what she'd been learning about God through the story of another sufferer. She pulls her study Bible down from the shelf behind her and turns the pages to Ruth 1:13b, reading the verse in which Naomi, after the deaths of her husband and two sons, states: *the hand of the Lord has gone out against me.*

In the study notes, Sara says, she remembers reading the following: *Naomi is interpreting her hard circumstances as coming from God's enmity toward her; as the rest of the book will make plain, she is mistaken.*[10] This explanation helped Sara see that her miscarriages were not a sign of God's judgment, but rather that even in the midst of them, He was being kind to her. She saw God's presence as very near, in the form of friends and family who brought meals, watched Asher, and even bought Sara new clothes to help cheer her up.

It wasn't long before Sara was pregnant again, and nine months later, after another healthy pregnancy, she gave birth to Abby.

With two miscarriages and two births, the Brodes still wanted more children and had no real reason to suspect a problem.

"I think the third [miscarriage] was a real turning point," Sara says. "That was kind of earth-shattering in the sense that I knew something was wrong with me."

Like Sara's second miscarriage, the third loss happened sometime late in the first trimester or early in the second. Justin and Sara had gone in for a routine checkup at fifteen or sixteen weeks. Sara's mom was with them, as were Asher and Abby, who were four and one and a half at the time. Their obstetrician was having trouble finding a heartbeat with the Doppler, so he sent them to get a sonogram, reassuring them that everything was fine.

"I had no fear whatsoever," Sara says. "I didn't think anything was wrong. I mean who has that kind of luck that something would be wrong again?" She laughs wryly.

When the doctor came in to tell them their baby had no heartbeat, Sara simply couldn't believe it. "How could that be?" she remembers saying.

Again, Sara had a D&C, but this time, she found it much more difficult to recover mentally and emotionally. "I remember being . . . more fearful right away," she says. "You think, *There's something really wrong with me, and how many more times is this going to happen?*"

At first, Sara remembers feeling "weird . . . like the world around me or something had changed."

Within a few weeks, though, she was experiencing severe anxiety and panic attacks. She and Justin had planned to celebrate their anniversary while Asher and Abby stayed with their grandparents, but Sara's symptoms became so intense she no longer knew how to manage them.

10. *ESV Study Bible*, 479.

She recalls looking out the window into her backyard and "having these terrible thoughts like, *This is what the house would be like if the kids were dead.*" She felt a sudden, urgent need to go pick them up, even though doing so meant a four-hour drive. Justin helped her pack the car, and they began the drive, only to turn around after five minutes when Sara realized they'd forgotten something.

"I didn't know what to do with myself," Sara says.

She lay down for a bit, and then they decided to go to Outback for dinner. Sara couldn't even sit still. "We were trying to talk and have a good time," she recalls, "and I was just so fearful and anxious and like claustrophobic . . . I'm getting up from the table, coming back to the table, going to the bathroom, coming back, going outside the restaurant, calling my mom, pacing in the parking lot."

At one point she called her obstetrician's office, but she can't remember what they told her or if they prescribed her anything. What she recalls the most clearly were her feelings of panic. "It's like you're walking around in a nightmare," Sara says. "You need to run away and get out of your skin, and you don't know what to do."

"I'd never seen her like that," Justin confesses, "so I didn't know what to do with her either."

As they talk, I recall an experience I haven't thought about in some time, an anniversary trip CJ and I took to New York City about a month and a half after we'd lost Avaleen. We left Ellie with my parents on a Friday afternoon and drove into the city, arriving in the early evening. In our hotel room, dozens of stories high, I held back from the window, strangely dizzy and fearful, unable to enjoy the view I knew should have registered in my brain as spectacular. As the darkness of night settled, I felt increasingly afraid, the busy, pulsing streets filling my mind with a vague and restless terror. Like Sara, I felt a visceral desire to escape my own body, and I panicked about being away from Ellie, suddenly certain I would lose her too. For me, the terror subsided by Saturday morning, when I simply felt sad. All I wanted to do was sit and cry, but I allowed CJ to hold my arm and guide me through the city streets, my tears steady behind my sunglasses.

For Sara, however, the experience of intense anxiety she now believes to be post-traumatic stress disorder continued for months.

"That summer was pretty terrible," Justin says.

"It was awful," Sara agrees. "It was an awful, awful time."

Sara would often wake in the middle of the night with panic attacks, sometimes so intense that she would vomit. "It was like my mind was always racing, *What bad thing is going to happen next?*" she says. "*Are the kids going to die? Is Justin going to die? What's going to happen?*"

A physician's assistant at her psychiatry office put her on a medication to help with the anxiety, and though it calmed her panic, Sara still didn't feel like herself. She recalls a lake house vacation that summer. "It was like everybody around me was laughing and having a good time. The kids were in the water splashing. It's sunny, beautiful weather, and I felt like I was in a snow globe or something. I couldn't engage . . . I felt peaceful I guess in some way, but I was not happy."

"I really had no idea what to do other than pray for her, help her, try to reassure her," Justin says. "I didn't really have much experience at all with anything like that."

Justin and Sara had several friends from church, including a pastor and a pastor's wife, who'd dealt with anxiety and depression themselves and were able to care for them during this time. Eventually, Sara was able to see a psychiatrist who prescribed medications that enabled her feel more like herself, and she also went to see a counselor, who helped arm her with new coping skills to manage the anxiety in conjunction with the medication.

Still, Sara's brush with mental illness had a profound impact. "That was probably the worst time of my life, ever," she reflects. "I would have five more miscarriages if it meant never having mental health problems again. It was the worst thing, and I never knew how bad it is."

Both she and Justin have a new and deep compassion for those who face mental health issues on an ongoing basis. Sara says she's less quick to judge others and the way they're handling things. "You just don't know until you've been in somebody's shoes what they've got going on," she says. "Most of us are just doing our best."

The Brodes are thankful for a church family who responded to their crisis with understanding, especially since they know some Christians would attribute mental illness to the absence of belief in God. "They might think you just need to have a little more faith," Sara says, "as though it's something you can control. That was definitely not something I could control. If you could control crazy, you would."

In spite of, and perhaps because of, her own lack of control, Sara feels her battle with anxiety was used by God to deepen her understanding of faith and grace. During her struggles, she recalls telling one of her friends that she didn't think she would ever be the same again. The friend replied, "You know what? You're not going to be the same. But you're going to be more like Christ."

Now a few years removed from the intensity of her distress, Sara can see how this is true. But in her panic, she found it difficult to hold on to God. "All I could do," she says, "was read His word, say it back to Him." Her prayers, she remembers, went something like this, "Okay, you're going to deliver me. Like, do it. Please."

Through her experiences, though, she began to learn what faith really is. "You're just holding on to Jesus with the tiniest bit of strength, the tiniest, tiniest bit, and all you can do is hold on and ask Him to deliver you and not let go."

I know what she means, can recall the many days in the months after losing Avaleen where all I could do was simply sob, "*I don't understand God. Why? Why?*" At the time, I didn't think of it as prayer, but listening to Sara, I realize it was. I was making my own feeble cries for help to the God I couldn't feel or see.

For the Brodes, any plans for another pregnancy were put on hold as they focused on helping Sara get better. Sara, now fully convinced that something was wrong with her body, also used the time after the third miscarriage to begin exploring additional fertility testing and treatment. Though her two most recent miscarriages had likely occurred sometime late in the first trimester, her obstetrician hadn't been able to grow tissue from the babies to test for any sort of genetic defects or problems.

Since he couldn't provide any further help, he referred her to a local maternal-fetal medicine specialist. This specialist ran a battery of tests, including a karyotype, which examined Justin and Sara's chromosomes to see if they were predisposed to produce babies with genetic abnormalities. None of their test results revealed any issues.

Sara felt frustrated by the lack of information for people like her, people who could get pregnant easily, but who experienced repeated miscarriages. "You find a lot about infertility," she says. "There's tons of infertility clinics, but not a lot of them focus on recurrent miscarriage."

A friend referred her to a fertility clinic in nearby Pittsburgh. The specialist there ordered one additional test to rule out any abnormalities with the structure of Sara's uterus. When that test result also came back normal, the specialist had nothing further to offer the Brodes. "She used the word *crude*," Sara remembers. "She said, 'Our knowledge is still very crude in a lot of this, and basically we just don't know." Her recommendation was to just keep trying."

Unsatisfied, Sara turned to an integrative medicine clinic where the practitioners blended Western and alternative approaches to treat various health problems. "That place was really, really cool," she says.

"That's cute that you call it cool," Justin laughs.

"It *was* cool though," Sara retorts. "They were showing *Food, Inc.* on the DVD player when you sit in the lobby and wait."

"There's not much cooler than that," Justin teases.

I smile too, noting—as I have at several points throughout the evening—how much peace and laughter exists between the two of them, remarkable traits given all they've experienced.

Sara explains that the doctor she saw at the clinic ordered extensive testing on hormones and food sensitivities and reported "a lot of things that were slightly out of whack" with her body, including a gluten intolerance. At the same time, she says, she'd come across several articles establishing a connection between gluten sensitivity and miscarriage. "I thought, *It's the gluten!* That's it. Going off gluten is going to solve my problems. I'm not going to miscarry."

Soon after this discovery, Sara learned she was pregnant again. However, just a few days later, at five and a half weeks, she began to bleed. Both she and Justin remember feeling sad, but because the loss was so early, they didn't find it as difficult as some of their previous miscarriages. In addition, because Sara hadn't finished ironing out all of the issues the integrative health practitioner had noted, she hoped doing so would help her carry a future pregnancy to term.

Within a few months, with all known health issues under control, Sara learned she was pregnant again. "I thought . . . *I'm going to be in a lot better place now*," she says.

However, at ten weeks, Sara miscarried for the fifth time and had to endure another D&C. She was still on her anti-depressant at that time, and thankfully her anxiety did not return. She turned her grief toward research, reading books and scouring the internet for a specialist who might be able to help her. After uncovering information about new research indicating recurrent miscarriages can be caused by immunological factors, she returned to the specialist in Pittsburgh, research in arm, to see if she could find answers.

Instead, the specialist refused to look at her book and handed her a packet of protocols for treating women with recurrent miscarriages released in 2001 by the American College of OBGYNs. "She hands me this Xeroxed copy of information that's eleven years old?" Sara says incredulously, her voice rising with passion. "And this is what I'm being treated with? That's unacceptable. That is ancient times in the medical field."

I know the rest of the story because I've been living it with Sara over the past year: her blog, her visits to the specialist we've both seen, the past few months of injections and medications and trying once again for a baby.

I admire Justin and Sara's tenacity, the faith they have to persevere. I'm not sure I'd be able to do so after another miscarriage, let alone four. I wonder what sustains them, why they haven't decided to stop trying for another baby or to pursue adoption. I hesitate, not wanting to come across as judgmental, but I decide to ask. "Why not quit?"

"We've come so far," Sara says. "Finding [the specialist] and all this new information that I never knew existed . . . it just feels like it's right around the corner. But," she continues, "I'm not pregnant. We're still trying."

I sense the frustration in her voice, and like my interview with Jared and Kim, I feel uncomfortable about my own pregnancy. I don't understand why God would lead her and Justin through all of these trials to someone who can finally help them and then deny them a pregnancy.

"Where do you see God in all this?" I ask, aware of the obvious places where it must be difficult to do so.

"For me," Justin says, "the most clear thing is how much I love Sara and how strong I believe our marriage is now compared to where it first started." He continues, "I trust that God would've grown our marriage if everything had turned out just fine and we had four kids by now, but I really believe He did some work through all this."

"I'm more myself," Sara says simply. "I'm more willing to try things and take risks."

As they continue to reflect on how their experience has changed them, it becomes clear God has shown each of them His deep love in spite of their doubts and the anger they've felt toward Him at times. Justin recalls a particular season in the midst of the miscarriages and after the death of his brother where he was angry at God, even though he's not sure he realized it at the time. "I can fully trust that He knew exactly where I was," Justin says, "and still applied Jesus's blood to my life."

Sara too feels she has a much deeper understanding of God's grace and patience. "There's been so much that we've been through now," she says. "There's no way anybody could go through it and respond perfectly. Only Christ did that, and I'm getting that now. God loves us anyway, no matter if we respond perfectly to things or if we don't."

This makes sense to me. My own grief and anger and questions about God have torn down the illusions I once had of being a faith-filled Christian marching victoriously through life. I've had little to offer and I haven't even been sure of what I believe half the time. Still, miraculously, God remains present and involved in my life. And so, though I often wish I didn't deal with doubt, I'm also grateful for it, for the way it's helped me understand grace on a deeper level.

———

I wake up the next morning to begin the long drive home so that I can make it back for a women's small group meeting I'm hosting in the afternoon. I'm nearing the twelve-week point in this pregnancy, the point where most people consider their risk of miscarriage as having passed, and I want to tell the ladies in my small group that I'm pregnant, ask them to pray for me, and share my fear of losing another baby in the second trimester.

I lead the meeting, facilitating opportunities for others to talk about their lives, but things are wrapping up before I work up the courage to offer my own need. "Can I share one quick prayer request?" I ask, not wanting to keep anyone later than the allotted time.

My "quick" request turns into a half-hour of pouring out my heart: my good news and my fears, especially as I approach the point in my pregnancy when we lost Avaleen. Sara's story is fresh in my mind, and I tell the group that I don't think my faith would survive another loss.

"How would you define faith?" one woman asks.

I pause. The words that come out of my mouth surprise me. "I guess I'd say it's the choice to keep coming back to God even when you don't understand or feel like you really believe," I say through tears. I know even as I'm speaking that my definition last year would have been different. It would have included words like *confidence* and *assurance*, words that now feel beyond my grasp. This is an important shift, I realize. I'm beginning to understand something pivotal about the Christian walk and the true nature of faith in suffering.

In that moment, I don't see the obvious connection between my changing definition of faith and the Brodes's story. I don't realize the way the stories of all the families I've been talking with are shaping me. I simply taste a small bit of hope that maybe all of the fears and doubts I carry with this pregnancy are not a sign of my lack of belief, but rather the place where my faith is truly beginning to grow.

I've learned something surprising these past few months in the midst of my undisciplined wandering—even without setting aside time to seek Him, God speaks. I can't tell you particular verses that have been meaningful to me lately or a specific prayer God has answered this month, but I can tell you this: I see God's hand all over my life, in places I haven't been able to see Him for a long time. I have renewed confidence that He has a good plan for me and that even when neither He nor His plan can be seen in the darkness, He's there all the same.

—Blog post, June 28, 2013

Chapter 9

JUNE: SCOTT AND CHRISTINE

The sun is bright as I sit in my beach chair, watching CJ and Ellie run in the surf. I'm tired and continue to feel nauseous at times, but I'm sixteen weeks pregnant now—past the point in the pregnancy when we lost Avaleen. The grip of my anxiety has begun to loosen.

Still, I think often of the baby we never met. We're at the beach today to remember her and celebrate her, just as we did one year ago. We've decided to make this day trip an annual tradition, a way to include our second daughter as part of the ongoing story of our family.

I bury my toes into the warm sand and watch CJ and Ellie fill their buckets with ocean water. Inside me, I feel the twitches and turns of a baby very much alive.

Later, after naps and dinner, the sky's brightness begins to fade. CJ and I stand on the shoreline. He holds Ellie, and I rest one hand on my stomach. Waves crash around our feet, but we look beyond, where peaceful expanses of blue stretch to the horizon. CJ prays, "Thank you for Avaleen and her life. Please take good care of her for us."

The tears come, and I don't try to hold them back. I cry for what I've lost, and I cry too for what I've been given. I feel, quite simply, full. Full and grateful. Grateful for the gift of Avaleen—as much as her loss continues to grieve me—and grateful for my husband, my daughter, and this new life growing inside me.

Far as the Curse Is Found

But even as the weeks pass and the odds of this baby's survival continue to improve, I can't stop worrying. It isn't the paralyzing sort of worry I knew in the early days, the kind that tied my stomach in knots or made my chest so tight I could scarcely breathe. It's simply the constant awareness of life's fragility, the knowledge that at any moment, this baby could be gone.

From time to time throughout the day, I'll realize I haven't felt movement, and I'll think, *It happened.* I'll imagine calling the doctor, and—ever the planner—I'll spend a moment trying to figure out how a D&E will fit into my schedule over the next few days. And then, minutes later, I'll note a flutter or a kick, and I'll move on with what I'm doing. Moments like this happen with such frequency I hardly notice them anymore. With their regularity, they've lost any sort of emotional intensity. For me, the possibility of this baby's death is as much a part of my reality as his or her life.

———

I meet Scott and Christine Lee at their single-family brick home in an affluent Northern Virginia suburb. Scott answers the door with a warm smile. "Congratulations!" he says.

I thank him, smiling too, but I can't help but think, as I do every time someone expresses joy about this pregnancy, that I hope it isn't premature to be excited.

Inside, I meet eight-month-old Marissa, a chubby bundle of cuteness, and Sasha, the family's friendly husky mix. I pet Sasha and watch Marissa roll and grab and bang, and I try to remember what it was like to have a baby in my home. It seems so long ago that Ellie was this age, and it's hard to imagine that in a few months, I might really bring home another baby from the hospital.

While Marissa plays, I talk with Scott and Christine, old acquaintances a mutual friend reconnected me with after learning of this book project. Scott, clad in mesh shorts and a blue triathlon shirt, tells me about the event he'll be participating in early the next morning. I'm both surprised and thankful that he's willing to do this interview the night before a big race.

"How did you get into doing triathlons?" I ask.

I'm not expecting his answer. "I think it was actually after one of the miscarriages," he says. "I was looking for an escape."

Christine will be a spectator tomorrow but tells me that before her pregnancy with Marissa, she competed in a triathlon too. She'd like to do more.

Scott prepares a delicious pre-race dinner: pasta with tomato sauce and grilled chicken. Afterward, Christine puts Marissa to bed, and then the three of us gather in their living room to talk. Scott sits cross-legged on the beige wall-to-wall carpeting, sipping a cup of tea. On the other side of Marisa's colorful play mat, Christine also settles on the floor, explaining that it's more comfortable for her back. I opt for the couch.

Scott and Christine are both Korean-American. Christine grew up just miles away in another Northern Virginia suburb. Her childhood, like those of many of my Korean-American friends, was steeped in Christianity. Her father helped start one of the prominent Korean congregations in the area, and he continues to serve as a church elder. "I was saved in sixth grade," she says, "but didn't make it a serious thing until maybe ninth." In high school and in college, she was actively involved in Christian community, serving as a worship leader and small group coordinator.

Scott, on the other hand, grew up in New York and never attended church with his parents. In middle school, however, his parents sent him to Camp Good News in Cape Cod, Massachusetts. Family friends had recommended this camp, which happened to be Christian. Scott returned there year after year, and one summer, he decided to commit his life to Christ. However, because he had "no support structure at home," it wasn't until college that he began attending church regularly.

Incidentally, college is also where Scott and Christine met, during the week of Scott's freshmen orientation at Carnegie Mellon. Their first encounter was on the basketball court, where Scott was immediately attracted to Christine and impressed by her athleticism. "You don't see a lot of girls playing basketball," he says.

Christine, a year older than Scott, wasn't interested. "I figured he was a freshman," she says, "so I was like, 'Not an option!'"

"She actually forgot my name the second time we ran into each other," Scott interjects. "I [gave] her a clue, and I thought I was being smooth." He told her, "You can find me in the bathroom," but says Christine was confused. "She's like, 'John?'" Scott laughs at the memory.

"But then after he said that," Christine explains, "I saw his name everywhere because of Scott tissue."

In spite of Christine's initial reluctance, she spent a lot of time with Scott that year, and by September of the following year, the two were an official pair. They dated for their remaining college years and both settled in the DC area after graduation, pursuing careers in IT. Two years after Scott's graduation, they married.

While neither Scott nor Christine was in a rush to have kids, they both knew they wanted them. Christine had dreams of a large family. "I grew up with a lot of cousins," she says, "so [they] were like brothers and sisters and we spent a lot of time together . . . I wanted that for our kids."

Initially, Scott wasn't so sure, but as time passed, he began to see the value in a large family. He references the television show *Parenthood* as a factor that influenced his thinking. The show features four grown siblings who live in the same small town and walk through the ups and downs of life together. "There was one scene where all the siblings were sitting at a table just supporting each other," Scott says. "I think that's pretty cool."

Still, he and Christine decided to wait until a few years before going off of birth control. Then, Scott explains, we "kind of let nature take its course."

Two months later, Christine was pregnant. "I was really excited, and I was actually kind of scared too," she says. "All my life, things were really calculated, and what I wanted to achieve, I always got. In my mind, I wanted to be married by the time I was twenty-five. I wanted to have a baby by the time I was twenty-eight. And I was twenty-eight."

At Christine's ten-week appointment, however, she knew something was wrong when the nurse checking for the baby's heartbeat suddenly became "really nice." An ultrasound at the hospital revealed the pregnancy wasn't progressing as it should have. "It was kind of small," Scott says, "and there was no yolk sac."

Still processing this news, Scott and Christine went to church that Sunday. They hadn't told anyone there they were pregnant, and as it happened, on that morning another couple announced they were expecting twins.

"We couldn't stay because it was too emotional," Scott says.

"I started bawling," Christine adds.

A few hours later, Christine miscarried at home. "I felt just really sad and devastated."

She worried she'd done something to cause the miscarriage. Before finding out she was pregnant, she'd taken painkillers for her sciatica. "I also had a glass of wine at somebody's wedding," she says. "There was a lot of stuff to feel guilty for."

I'm sure Christine read the same information I did when I was desperate to figure out why Avaleen died. I'm sure she knows that, according to the American College of Obstetricians and Gynecologists, chromosomal abnormalities account for roughly half of early pregnancy losses and that small amounts of alcohol and caffeine are unlikely to lead to miscarriage.[11] But I understand her feelings of guilt—I felt them too. I couldn't stop thinking about how my baby had died inside me, how I must somehow have been at fault.

Initially, Scott focused all his energies on caring for Christine. "I was almost on autopilot," he says, "trying to make sure Christine was okay and that I was there and she had everything she needed."

As time passed, however, Scott allowed himself to feel his own emotions. "I guess," he says, "I felt empty and to some degree somewhat angry that this could happen."

Everyone kept telling them that things happen for a reason, that their baby wasn't meant to be. While grieving, Scott and Christine believed them. They decided to try again.

Six months after the miscarriage, Christine learned she was pregnant. "I was happy," Scott says, "and I was confident we were going to have a baby."

Because she feared she'd somehow caused the previous miscarriage, Christine was extra cautious this time around. "I wasn't doing anything wrong at all," she says. "I made an approved list; I'm only eating from this. I slept as much as I could."

I see myself in her words: the anxiety, the desire to prevent more heartache, the need to control. Even as I religiously avoid caffeine and dairy and keep up with my regimen of supplements, I remind myself that people smoke and drink and do drugs and eat terribly during their pregnancies and still give birth to healthy babies. But I can't stop feeling afraid that somehow a choice I make will end the life inside of me.

Christine was encouraged by seeing a yolk sac during an ultrasound and by the morning sickness everyone promised her was a good sign. "Everything was perfect," Christine says, "and still . . ." She trails off.

She miscarried her second baby at eight weeks gestation.

This time, Christine's grief raised deep questions in her soul. "I think everyone expected me to be angry," she says. "I think it was more that I felt betrayed by God. I was like, 'How could you let this happen?' I also kept thinking that I did all the right things that I felt a Christian should do, and

11. The American College of Obstetricians and Gynecologists, "Early Pregnancy Loss," 1–2.

I was also a worship leader. I waited until marriage to have sex, and this is how I get repaid?"

From where she's sitting on the floor, Christine reaches her hands toward her toes, stretching. She's calm now, but I know the inner turmoil she's describing was anything but peaceful. "I was definitely angry," Scott says.

"Yeah, you were," Christine agrees. "It was hard for me to go to church and worship after that happened," says Scott. "I'd sit there . . . hearing what was happening but not really focusing on it, just being there."

Church can be an uncomfortable place when God is distant, when singing peppy praise songs or making small talk is the last thing you feel like doing. Scott and Christine both acknowledge that if it weren't for Christine's insistence on attendance, Scott probably would have stopped going altogether.

"I don't know why I felt the need to go," she says. "I think I was scared of abandoning God, but I didn't want to go either."

To make matters more complicated, Scott and Christine's congregation disbanded around this time, and they found themselves forced to look for a new church home.

"I was questioning myself," Christine says. "*Is this it? Is this the point when I don't become a Christian anymore?* And what was weird was I felt everyone else kind of assumed that I was being strong about it . . . and my faith was getting stronger . . . but secretly I'm like, *I don't know if I can do this anymore. If this is what God is like, then I don't want to be part of it.*"

Scott and Christine began seeing a Christian counselor. At her encouragement, they named their babies, a step that initially felt scary to Christine, but ended up helping her and Scott feel a sense of closure.

In an effort to prevent more miscarriages, they also pursued various fertility tests and genetic counseling, as well as seeing an acupuncturist. "I was actually hopeful for the tests," Christine says, "because I was like, *Okay, let's figure out what's wrong and fix it.*"

"That was the most frustrating part," Scott recalls. The doctors all told them the same thing, he recounts, "You guys are healthy individuals with no genetic issues.'"

Desperate for answers, they saw one specialist who blamed their losses on Christine's high-carb diet and encouraged her to cut back on starches and sugars during her next pregnancy. They also saw a Korean herbalist who had Christine drink an herbal concoction for three weeks.

"If you smelled it, you'd throw up," Christine says. "It was so disgusting."

In spite of these remedies, and in spite of seeing the heartbeat of their third baby, Christine had yet another miscarriage. This time, the baby was seven weeks along.

Reeling, the couple took off three weeks from their respective jobs and headed to the Southwest, visiting Phoenix, Sedona, Las Vegas, San Diego, and Los Angeles. "We could look back on it," Scott says, "and see that we were running away from facing reality."

But the reality was there when they returned, inescapable. For both Scott and Christine, their struggles with God intensified with each miscarriage. "I think it got harder and harder to be faithful [to God]," Scott says. "The anger continued to grow."

And there were other challenges. Many of the people around Scott and Christine knew nothing of their difficulties. The couple was established and successful in their careers; they'd purchased a family home and car. From the outside, it looked like everything was ready for them to grow their family. "Everyone was like, 'You've been married for how long and you don't have kids?'" Scott recalls. "It's like, *Oh my gosh! Shut up already.*"

They told people they were in no rush, that their jobs kept them busy. "But really," Christine says, "my career advancing was a byproduct of what we were going through."

They also found it difficult when friends announced pregnancies. "There was this sick side of me," Christine says. She remembers thinking, "I wonder if they're going to feel a loss like us."

I recall thinking similarly after Avaleen's death. Pregnancy announcements made me envious, but I also disliked how they were generally presented with unbridled optimism. *Don't you know how fragile this life is? I* wanted to scream. *Don't you know that tragedy might strike, just like it struck me?*

Christine was helped by the lyrics of a hymn called "Be Still, My Soul," which had been sent to her by a family member. She loved the whole hymn but was drawn in particular to these lines: "*Be still, my soul: your best, your heavenly Friend through thorny ways leads to a joyful end. Be still, my soul: your God will undertake to guide the future as He has the past. Your hope, your confidence let nothing shake; all now mysterious shall be bright at last.*"[12] The words reminded her God had been faithful to her in the past and that His faithfulness would not change.

---

12. Von Schlegel, "Be Still My Soul," lines 5–10.

Scott and Christine clung to this truth as they kept trying to get pregnant. They saw a specialist at George Washington Hospital who told them that based on their history, they had a one in five chance of carrying a baby to term. "She was like, 'I know it sounds disheartening, but just keep trying. And it should happen one day,'" Christine explains.

They followed her advice, and, because they felt disconnected from God themselves and because they hadn't met many people at their new church, they asked others to pray for them, building an e-mail prayer team of close friends. "Because I couldn't hear God," Christine says, "I was like someone else can hear God for us."

As Christine talks, I picture the friends described in the Gospel of Luke, who lowered their paralyzed friend down through the roof to get him to Jesus.[13] I think, with a deep sense of gratitude, of all the friends who have prayed for us and for the baby inside of me. And I think too of the faith Christine displayed in asking others to pray, even when she wasn't sure how she felt about God.

Almost a year after her third miscarriage, Christine lost yet another baby. Scott recalls her waking him in the middle of the night, telling him she was miscarrying and asking him to call the doctor for instructions. This time, they wanted to save the baby's body in hopes that laboratory testing would shed some light on their recurrent losses. "I broke down," Scott says, recalling the difficulty of that process: "That was really hard to . . . see whatever was in there . . . To me, it was the baby. To put it on ice and send it off was very difficult."

I think back to Sara's story of passing her first baby in the toilet and not wanting to look and of my desire to avoid handling Avaleen's dead body on my own. I admire Scott's courage.

Unfortunately, the lab tests yielded no results. And so Scott and Christine simply tried again, hoping the specialist was right, that eventually Christine would be able to carry a baby to term. In the meantime, they decided to join a small group at their new church.

When Christine found out she was pregnant for the fifth time, she and Scott felt ready to share their story with their new small group. During one meeting when the leader asked for prayer requests, Christine announced that she was pregnant. People began congratulating her and Scott but grew quiet when they realized she was crying. After the couple shared about

13. Luke 5:18-19.

their miscarriages, the group prayed for them, both that night and as the pregnancy progressed.

That support meant a lot to both of them. "It was definitely freeing," Christine says of the choice to share their story with the group.

Early in this pregnancy, Christine experienced some spotting and was convinced she was losing this baby too. "So I picked up my guitar and started worshipping and begging God not to do it again," Christine says, her voice breaking and her eyes brimming with tears. She pauses. "I thought, 'If He hears me this time, then I promise to be more faithful.'"

I know, as does Christine, that God doesn't work this way, that He doesn't cause miscarriages because of our lack of faithfulness, that He doesn't prevent them because we finally offer the right bargaining chip. But I understand her desperate prayer. It's the honest cry of a mother who would do anything for her child, a plea from the depths of her soul. I too have prayed these kinds of prayers, and in a strange way, I suspect that they honor God as much as and perhaps more than the theologically pristine prayers I often try to create.

Christine didn't feel like she got an answer from God, and the spotting continued for several more days. But then it stopped, and the pregnancy continued to progress without any other troubling symptoms. Because of their history, however, both she and Scott worried a lot. "After every ultrasound," Scott says, "I felt like I was going to get bad news."

In the second trimester, Christine's obstetrician feared her cervix was opening and sent her to a maternal-fetal specialist, who ordered her to strictly limit her lifting and walking. Even though she'd never tested positive for any clotting disorders, she took low-dose aspirin because specialists told her "it couldn't hurt."

Whether or not any of these things helped, Scott and Christine will never know, but in the fall of 2012, Marissa Jiyun was born, perfect and healthy. It was a happy moment for Scott and Christine. "I admitted to Christine later that I did shed a tear," Scott jokes.

And yet, even leading up to Marissa's birth, Christine experienced a reminder of her miscarriages. "The labor pains were very similar to the miscarriage pains," she says. "Near the end, it was a sobering thought: . . . *I recognize these pains.*"

She also continued to experience fear and anxiety after Marissa's birth. "I would stare at the monitor," she recalls. "Any kind of peep she made I jumped out of bed . . . I had this fear that somebody was going to try to take her from us."

I glance at my phone to check the time. We've been talking for nearly two hours, and I'm trying to stay mindful of Scott's early morning race. I narrow down my list of remaining questions. "Would you say Marissa's birth was a redemptive experience?" I ask, thinking of the baby growing inside of me, wondering what it might feel like to hold a living newborn again.

"I don't know," Christine ponders. "I'm definitely very thankful and joyful that Marissa's here and even . . . when it's the toughest, I still don't think it's that bad."

"I don't think there's a day that goes by that I don't think about our other babies," Scott clarifies. "I think it's easier for us, for me, to feel joy now that Marissa is here, but I still feel sad about our others because I constantly think, *Gosh, our first would have been like four or five.*"

"Yeah, we could have had five kids by now," Christine adds, her voice wistful. "I could've had my five."

Marissa's birth also didn't resolve all of their questions, doubt, and disconnect from God. Before her pregnancies, Christine says, "I could hear God's voice, and things were distinct. Now it's kind of fuzzy." She continues, "The last four or five years have been crippling to my faith."

She often feels like people around her expect her to have received some revelation from God now that Marissa has been born, a lesson learned from their trials, perhaps an explanation of what all the suffering was about.

But, both she and Scott agree, they don't know. "We're still figuring it out," Christine says.

They do find comfort in thinking about the big picture of history and God's redemptive work outside of our finite understanding of time. "God's time continuum is so different from what we go through as people on this Earth," Scott says, going on to explain that God did answer their prayers for a baby, even though the five years they waited felt like an eternity to them.

Christine reflects on a book she read by Anne Graham Lotz entitled *Why?* In it, Graham Lotz retells the Bible story of Lazarus and emphasizes the fact that there were several days between Lazarus's family calling for help and Jesus's arrival to raise him from the dead. During those days, Lazarus's family couldn't see where Jesus was and would have presumably felt, much like Scott and Christine did, abandoned by Him.[14] But for Lazarus,

14. Graham Lotz, *Why?*

and for Scott and Christine, He did eventually show up and answer their prayers.

They're right. There is comfort to be found in knowing that God's story is bigger than ours, that He is at work even when He can't be seen. But, in the days that follow our interview, I keep coming back to the corollary thought, one they shared over and over again: *we don't know*. We don't know what the point of our suffering is. We can't wrap it all up in a neat package and tell others why we had to go through it and exactly what we learned. There is much mystery surrounding God's purposes, especially as they relate to suffering.

I think back to my conversation with the Brodes last month and to my small group epiphany shortly thereafter, and I reflect again on the nature of faith. I think about Scott and Christine going to church when they didn't feel like it, when they were motivated by duty and fear more than desire or delight. I think about their family now, with the joy of their longed-for baby girl in their arms, but with the ongoing grief of four babies lost. I think of the miracle it is that they still long to hear God's voice, that even in the silence, they have confidence He will speak again one day. Here too, I see faith. Here too, I taste freedom to come to God as I am.

I'm pregnant. It's such a simple sentence, but writing it feels both exhilarating and scary, much like my hesitant jumps off the high dive when I was ten.

The link between pregnancy and having a baby has been severed, and I'm still finding it difficult to reestablish the connection. Telling the world is one way to choose to celebrate this life, to rejoice in this child who is right now very much alive, making her presence known with gentle flips and kicks while I write. I battle fear of losing this baby every day and probably will until she is safely in my arms, but I don't want to be consumed by that fear.

So I'm telling you all: I am pregnant—twenty weeks. We're delighted and terrified, grateful and hopeful.

—BLOG POST, JULY 16, 2013

Chapter 10

JULY: DAVE AND CATHY

I sit in the hospital waiting room, my palms sweaty, my heart racing. The last time I waited in this space was just over a year ago, when we needed an ultrasound to confirm that Avaleen had died.

CJ enters the waiting room, having parked our car, and takes a seat beside me. I reach for his hand. "I'm nervous," I say.

I keep reminding myself that this time is different. I feel this baby move on a regular basis and have been receiving ultrasounds at every appointment, all of which show a strong heartbeat and healthy fetal development. Still, something about being in a hospital, about the more in-depth scan that is about to be performed, sets me on edge. *What if they see a problem my doctor missed? What if, in spite of all the movement I've been feeling, there's no heartbeat—again?*

I search the room, studying the other women around me. I note the size of their bellies and their demeanor, trying to gauge the stage of their pregnancies and their reasons for being here today. *Are they all thinking about the gender reveal parties they have planned for later today?* I wonder. *Or are there others like me who wait nervously, knowing they may not leave with good news?*

A technician opens the waiting room door and calls my name. We follow her down the hallway into a dark examination room. I know the drill. I settle myself on the table and lift my shirt, revealing what I'm suddenly certain is a too-small bump. *Wasn't I bigger by this point with Ellie?* I think. *Maybe this baby isn't growing enough.*

As the technician spreads ultrasound gel on my stomach, she asks, "Do you want to know your baby's gender?"

I look at CJ. "Yes," we say together. She has no way of knowing that for us, this appointment is about so much more. We do want to know if we're having a boy or a girl, but really, we don't care. We just want to hear that our child is growing well, that he or she will be okay.

I inhale deeply as she takes the ultrasound wand in her hand and presses it against my belly. The form of a small body appears on the screen. "It's a girl," she says immediately, almost before I have a chance to register the comforting rhythm of a heartbeat.

We smile, excited. Ellie's been insistent that she's having a baby sister, and both of us have wanted that for her. I can't wait to tell her. But I hold my breath while the technician continues her scan, taking photos of our little girl's heart and head and limbs. I'm comforted by the assuring sound of a steady heartbeat, but I know there are many other things that might be wrong. I also know the technician won't be the one to tell us, so I watch her face for clues. She's brisk and matter-of-fact, which I hope is a good sign.

After the tech is finished, CJ and I sit in an empty office, waiting for a doctor to read us the results. It's all eerily familiar. We sat in this same room, or one identical to it, during my pregnancy with Ellie and then again after Avaleen died. Today, when the doctor enters, she is bright and cheerful. "Everything looks completely normal and perfect," she tells us warmly.

After she explains the baby's measurements and her position in my uterus, CJ and I leave the office, walking together down the hallway and back through the waiting room toward the hospital lobby. I can't hold it together any longer. I grip CJ's hand tightly, tears streaming down my face. I feel curious eyes upon us and worry observant onlookers might think we've received bad news. But I can't make the tears stop.

We're really having a baby, I think. *Another girl. And she's okay. She's really okay.*

———

I've scheduled an interview for the following day with Dave and Cathy Bowman, the couple who led the Navigators campus ministry I was involved with at Penn State. Roughly the same age as my parents, they welcomed me into their home and hearts as an eager and awkward freshman, and they drew upon decades of full-time college ministry experience in mentoring me and praying for me through my senior year and beyond.

They still live in State College, but we're in Lancaster for a Navigators reunion, so we decide to talk there. Rather than meeting them in a hotel lobby or at a restaurant, we opt for the quietest and most private place I can think of, the home of a neighbor of my parents, a couple I've known my entire life. They left me a key before heading out for the afternoon, and so with CJ and Ellie settled at my parents', the Bowmans and I make ourselves comfortable in the living room.

A fountain runs in the background, and we munch on carrots and hummus, crackers, grapes, and cheese while I tell them about my ultrasound appointment. Parents of two grown daughters themselves, they're thrilled to hear we're having another girl.

Gradually, our conversation shifts to infertility and miscarriage. To talk with Dave and Cathy, perhaps the kindest and most genuine people I've ever met, is to realize just how deeply invested they are in the lives of hundreds, perhaps thousands, of students and staff members they've poured their lives into over thirty-five plus years of campus ministry. Reproductive loss is a topic close to their hearts not only because of their own experiences, but also because they've spent decades praying for and walking with other staff couples and former students through infertility, miscarriage, and stillbirth.

"We know so many people," Cathy says. "For so many, we're just praying every week with them."

I nod, thinking about the countless times over the past fifteen years Cathy's made it a point to tell me she's been praying for me. My college friends and I used to joke that if Cathy was praying for something, it would happen. We once called her during a Penn State football game to ask her to pray against the opposing team. Penn State won.

I know Cathy to be an amazing friend and prayer warrior, but today, I want to hear her and Dave tell their own story.

"I grew up in a Christian family," Dave starts when I ask. "So I always heard about the Gospel. I knew everything and I believed it all, and so I decided on my own one night in bed. I just prayed and asked Christ to come into my life." He was seven years old at the time.

It wasn't until his involvement with the Navigators at Purdue University, however, that he developed a passion for mentoring others in their faith. Initially, Cathy says, laughing, "He was one of those guys who didn't do their Bible studies."

After "eighteen years of church and devotions," Dave explains, "I thought, *I don't know if there's anything else really to learn.*"

But when a friend he'd been talking to about Jesus made a profession of faith, Dave found himself suddenly interested in how to help that friend learn and grow as a Christian, a curiosity that eventually developed into his life's calling as a campus minister.

"How about you, Cathy?" I ask.

"I went to church all the time," she says, "taught Sunday school . . . but I never really understood where Jesus fit into the picture."

However, when she was a freshman, also at Purdue, her roommate got involved in a Bible study and began sharing verses and illustrations of the Gospel with Cathy. At first, Cathy says, "I thought, *Oh, that's good for her.*"

But late one night, when her roommate dragged her out of bed to practice sharing a visual illustration of the Gospel called the Bridge, Cathy found her previous understanding of Christianity destroyed.

I've seen the Bridge. It's a picture of a giant chasm with man on one side and God on the other, separated by sin. It illustrates the many ways people try and fail to bridge that gap and the miraculous solution Jesus worked through his death on the cross.

For Cathy, a self-described "good girl," it was the first time she realized she couldn't earn her salvation. She references a verse her roommate read that night, Eph 2:8–9, which says people are saved not by works, but by grace. "So I prayed and asked Christ into my life," says Cathy. "I had an ulcer at the time because I never could be good enough."

After that night, she never needed her ulcer medication again.

While both Dave and Cathy were involved with the Navigators at Purdue throughout their college years, they don't recall meeting until Dave's senior year, when Cathy, who was a year older and had already graduated, was a dietician in his dorm.

Cathy was working full time and leading the Navigator ministry to women on campus. "We were just friends," she says, a cracker in her hand. "I never thought of him as a possibility."

"I thought of her," Dave responds quickly, explaining how he was drawn to Cathy's heart for people. "She wanted to do the same things I wanted to do," he says. "She was involved in the same things I was involved in."

Like Cathy, Dave stayed at Purdue after graduation, taking on a full-time engineering job and spearheading a fraternity and sorority ministry on campus. "I once told him," Cathy says, "that if you tell me one more thing you're doing, I will refuse to believe you're human."

It took three years, but eventually Dave asked out Cathy, and she said yes. From there, things progressed quickly. Within four months, they were engaged and then married. Shortly before their wedding, they both quit their jobs, feeling called to ministry full time. After a brief honeymoon, they headed straight to a Navigator summer training program at Adrian College in Michigan, followed by a three-year staff training stint at Michigan State University.

I'm struck as I listen by just how large their capacities are, both individually and collectively. Everything about them is humble and unassuming, from the flannel shirts and blue jeans Dave's been wearing as long as I've known him to Cathy's large, round glasses and wide smile. They're so focused on others that it's easy to forget just how much they really do.

After their whirlwind courtship, the Bowmans spent the first few years of their marriage getting to know each other more deeply and enjoying their time as a couple while they continued to minister on campus. But children were always part of the plan; both Dave and Cathy wanted two or three.

Cathy was just shy of twenty-eight when they wed, and she remembers being fearful of not being able to get pregnant, knowing her own parents were married for twelve years before having children. Due to complications from a brain tumor her mother battled when Cathy was a child, her mother couldn't remember for sure why it had taken them so long. Cathy worried the delay was due to fertility problems of some kind.

However, when Dave and Cathy began trying, Cathy got pregnant quickly, not long before their second anniversary. A year and a half after their first daughter Lori was born, Cathy was pregnant again. Another little girl, Julia, was born without incident. "We thought, *Oh okay, our plan is going to be just fine*," Cathy says.

For several years after Julia's birth, though, Cathy was plagued with ongoing fatigue and constant sinus infections she now suspects were related to thyroid problems. "I think I was really depleted," she says.

Dave's cell phone rings, but he doesn't take the call. Cathy goes on, explaining that due to her health problems, she and Dave put plans for another pregnancy on hold. However, as Julia's second birthday neared, they felt ready to try again.

What happened next was totally unexpected, given the ease with which they'd birthed their first two children. Cathy could not get pregnant. With each of her girls, she'd conceived almost immediately, but this time, month after month passed without any success.

"It was hard," Cathy says. "I felt like crying every time my period came. It was like: *What's wrong? What's going on?*"

Dave and Cathy do not use this term, but I know that what the Bowmans were experiencing is a phenomenon known as secondary infertility, when a couple who has previously conceived without issue suddenly cannot. According to the National Infertility Association, 12 percent of American women deal with secondary infertility, and over half of all infertility cases fall in this category.[15]

For the Bowmans, a year passed without a pregnancy, then another. During this time, Cathy in particular began to feel God speaking to her, telling her that "two is going to be your quiver."

I nod, recognizing the verse she's referring to, an oft-quoted passage from Ps 127:3–5b: *Behold, children are a heritage from the Lord, the fruit of the womb a reward. Like arrows in the hand of a warrior are the children of one's youth. Blessed is the man who fills his quiver with them!*

"Was that a major thing for you to deal with?" I ask, wondering how I'd react if I sensed God telling me two kids was it for us. CJ and I think we want at least one more child after this pregnancy, and I know I would probably be disappointed if that didn't, or couldn't, happen.

"I kind of had some peace about it," Cathy says. "It wasn't hard for me. It was like, *Lord, you can direct it the way you want it.*"

Still, the Bowmans kept trying. Finally, after three years, Cathy found out she was pregnant. She was thirty-nine. "I was sort of surprised," Cathy says. "Very happy." She thought she must have been mistaken about her earlier sense from God.

"If I had a vote," she explains, "this is what I would have voted for."

---

15. RESOLVE: The National Infertility Association, "Myth about Secondary Infertility," lines 4–5.

From the beginning, however, the pregnancy was different. With her girls, Cathy had been sick in the first trimester, but this time, she wasn't. "I was thrilled!" Cathy says.

"I don't blame you," I smile, my own battle with long, difficult weeks of pregnancy-related nausea fresh. "I'd be thrilled too."

It was "not necessarily good," Dave interjects. "She was really sick with the other two."

At ten weeks, Cathy went to the doctor's office for a routine checkup. The doctor wanted her to get an ultrasound, a now routine procedure which she hadn't experienced with her earlier pregnancies.

During the ultrasound, Cathy says, "I could tell on the nurse's face that something was wrong." She asked if there was a problem, but the nurse refused to answer, saying the doctor would talk to Cathy later. "But I could tell," Cathy says.

Alone, she was comforted by a verse God brought to her mind immediately: Ps 84:11. She recites it from memory: *For the Lord God is a sun and a shield; the Lord bestows favor and honor. No good thing does he withhold from those who walk uprightly.*

I think back to my own moment alone in an ultrasound room. Unlike Cathy, I knew for certain that my baby was dead, but like her, God brought a verse to mind almost immediately.

Dave and Cathy had to wait until the following day before a doctor called to confirm what Cathy already sensed: their baby had died. "I cried for weeks," Cathy says, her voice wavering. "I could still cry."

"I cried too, with a group of guys the next day," Dave adds.

They also had to share the news with their girls, then six and four. "They were so excited," Cathy says. "They wanted a baby brother or sister."

"They both knew what was going on," Dave says.

Cathy finishes his thought, "So we had to answer all their questions: 'Where's our baby?'"

Two days after they received the news of their child's death, Cathy underwent a D&C. The months that followed were difficult, particularly for Cathy.

"I was very depressed," she explains. She'd been clinically depressed during the first trimesters of her other pregnancies and dealt with similar feelings of despair and hopelessness after the miscarriage.

For Dave, the emotions were simpler. "It's a big loss."

Cathy struggled especially when a close friend, also a mother of two, found out she was pregnant with a third and unexpected child. "She called her best friends around, and she was sobbing because she was pregnant," Cathy says. "And I was sobbing with her because I wanted to be."

Even today, Cathy says, when she sees pictures of her friend's son, she thinks about how old their third baby would be, what he or she would be like. "It still makes me cry," she admits.

I can relate. There's one particular acquaintance at church I often find it difficult to talk to, simply because her baby was born around the time Avaleen should have been. When we talk, I can't stop looking at her daughter with longing, trying to imagine what my own girl would be like at this age.

"It was so hard," Cathy says.

In spite of their profound grief, neither Dave nor Cathy remembers struggling with God or His goodness during this time. "I think He had sort of prepared my heart beforehand that two was going to be it for me," she says. "God has been so good to us."

Once again, I'm left marveling at how some people are able to experience suffering and not doubt God's existence or kindness. At every point in my life when I've faced a major difficulty, I've been left wrestling with God. I don't know any other way to walk with Him, to keep my heart alive to Him. I wonder what it would be like to know God in the way Cathy and Jim and some of the other people I've interviewed seem to, to simply believe that He is good no matter what.

For Dave, one passage in particular offered that kind of reassurance. Shortly after the miscarriage, he read the familiar words of Ps 139:13–16, the same passage that also comforted Mark and Lesley: *For you formed my inward parts; you knitted me together in my mother's womb. I praise you, for I am fearfully and wonderfully made. Wonderful are your works . . . Your eyes saw my unformed substance; in your book were written, every one of them, the days that were formed for me, when as yet there was none of them.*

Dave made a note in the margins of his Bible: *God is sovereign over our little one's death.*

For Cathy too, God's sovereign control over the life and death of their baby was comforting. She kept returning to the verse she'd received, almost audibly, in the ultrasound room moments after she knew their baby had died. "*No good things do you withhold,*" she repeats. "Okay, Lord."

I realize as I think about Cathy's words that her choice to keep returning to that verse, to keep saying *okay* to God in response, was likely her own way of wrestling through the difficult idea of God's sovereignty. I consider my own heart and how hard it often is for me to say okay to God, how I think I need to understand first. I remember what Mark said in my very first interview, about how Job repented of his quest to put God on the stand. *I'm not there yet,* I recognize. *Part of me is still trying to understand.*

For the Bowmans, as the months passed after the miscarriage, it became increasingly clear that they were finished trying to grow their family. At thirty-nine, Cathy was aware of the health problems her mother had faced in her forties, as well as the increasing risks of pregnancy complications. "I got rid of all my baby stuff," she says. "And then we were careful."

"It was a shift," Dave explains. As time went on, he says, they were more and more "used to just having two." The prospect of starting all over again became daunting.

They both found that they enjoyed their increasing freedom to pursue ministry opportunities on campus. Cathy in particular liked that as her girls got older, she was able to be a lot more involved with students. In a way, she says, the students filled the space in their hearts that had longed for more children. "I think we have had a lot more kids," she says, referring to the thousands of students they've ministered to over the years.

"Definitely," I affirm. I can think of dozens of people I know personally who consider the Bowmans second parents, and I know there must be hundreds more.

"I've always thought," Cathy says, "the mission He had for us would've been harder to do if we'd had more kids."

"Although there are some people on staff who have ten kids," Dave points out.

"I know," Cathy says. "And they can do it, but I'm not one. You know I'm not a multi-tasker."

She continues, "We're a team." Unlike other staff couples in which the wife focuses on childcare and the husband does all of the ministry, she explains, "We do it all together . . . Dave mops my floor; I type his letters."

They go on to recall how, when their girls were small, Cathy would spend Wednesday nights on campus while Dave stayed home. "We would play alligators," Dave remembers fondly.

"That was the kids' favorite night of the week," Cathy says. "I just feel like what He had for us is not what he had for everybody." She pauses. "Obviously."

She's right. It should be obvious that God's plans for the size and mission of each family are unique, but as I listen to Dave and Cathy, I think it hasn't always been obvious to me. I'd never been taught that birth control was wrong or that every Christian should have as large a family as possible, but I'd always admired the big families I knew. Even as a child, when I wouldn't have had words to explain it, I felt there was beauty in a love that spilled out, that kept on creating and welcoming new life. I couldn't understand why my parents didn't want more children. I planned to have seven.

I always thought this was a good desire, but listening to the Bowmans, I realize that somewhere along the way, these thoughts had grown beyond a desire to become a standard by which I measured "successful Christian families." In the past, I've silently judged other couples with small families, questioning their capacities and motives. And then, after losing Avaleen, I held myself against that same standard and felt like a second-tier mother. I feared that if Ellie were to be our only child, others would see me as somehow lesser because of my small family.

Even in my current state, with one toddler and a baby on the way, I'm aware of wanting more children. Perhaps that is a good, God-given longing, as I've always thought it to be. After all, the Bible does say children are a blessing from the Lord, and I believe that wholeheartedly. But I'm beginning to wonder if there isn't a dark side to my dreams of a large family, if my desires aren't tangled up with unhelpful comparisons, dangerous legalism, and my perpetual quest for success and achievement.

It's been tempting for me, I realize, to take that verse from Psalm 127 as license to pursue a large family without really bothering to seek God about it, to ask what He has for our family. I think of the Bowmans and of the beautiful things God has done in and through them, things that might not have been possible if they'd birthed more children. And I think of our own story so far, of how different our lives would be if Avaleen had been born. In all likelihood, there would be no interviews, no book, no third daughter now growing inside of me.

God gives, and God takes away. And sometimes, the giving and the taking are so intertwined that you can't see one without the other. In our finite, boundaried lives, the gift of children precludes other potential gifts, and the loss of children often leads to gifts that wouldn't be possible in their presence.

I don't like limits, and I don't like not being in control of choosing which gifts I am given. But there is freedom here too, if I can believe that God really is good, freedom to uncurl my fists and simply receive it all—Ellie's birth, Avaleen's death, this baby inside me—as gifts.

I'm trying to engage my heart . . . allowing myself the pleasure of planning for Baby Girl's arrival, allowing myself to dream of Ellie's new bedroom, of the simple nursery updates I'd like to make. I've booked a newborn photography session. I've started thinking about a birth plan.

But, still, just this morning, I woke up turning around a thought in my brain that felt both foreign and surprising: You have a baby inside of you. You're going to have a baby.

—BLOG POST, AUGUST 13, 2013

Chapter 11

AUGUST: CHRISTOPHER AND MARY GRACE

"Can I have a piece, Mommy?" Ellie asks, pointing to a miniature basket of assorted candies on the counter.

She's sitting in CJ's lap while I rest on the exam table, waiting for my OB. Now that we've passed the twenty-week point and feel more assurance about this baby's arrival, we've started bringing Ellie along to our appointments, hoping she'll begin to forge a connection with her little sister as we point to her movements on the ultrasound screen.

Ellie loves the whole experience: the child's lab coat she gets to try on in the waiting room, the fancy machine that dispenses cold water into tiny paper cups, the candy dishes on every counter, and the helium balloon she leaves holding. But she loves seeing her sister too. She's recently started calling her "Boo-bing," a name she's chosen for no clear reason other than the delight she feels in saying it. She repeats it over and over again, giggling, and I have to laugh along with her.

Our doctor enters the room. "Let's take a look at that baby," she says, her voice cheery. She begins the scan, and we all see her right away.

"Baby sister!" Ellie exclaims, pointing.

"Yes," I say. "There she is."

"She looks great," the doctor says. "Perfect."

In the weeks after my appointment, we enjoy the last days of summer. We drive to Pennsylvania to spend a weekend with my entire family, which now includes two nieces and a nephew. Then, back at home, I can peaches with a friend and pick out new dining room furniture. Life feels as I once thought it never again could—bright and full of promise. It's been a long journey to this place, and my joy, while genuine, makes me uncomfortable, as if the abatement of grief means my love for Avaleen is weakening.

I hate it when people ask me, as they often do, if I'm pregnant with my second child. In these moments, I feel torn between my desire to acknowledge Avaleen's life, to count her as one of my children, and the reality that trying to explain her to a stranger is complicated. I want to tell people about Avaleen, but I don't want to receive their pity or their awkward stares and comments.

"Yes," I usually answer simply, but I leave these exchanges with a lingering shame. I feel like a bad mother for keeping silent about the baby I lost, and I worry too that choosing not to talk about her means I'm somehow leaving her behind.

As August draws to a close, Ellie and I prepare to make a mid-week trip back to Pennsylvania for another interview. This time, I'll be talking with one of my closest friends and her husband, both of whom I've known since my freshmen year of college. Mary Grace and I roomed together our junior and senior years, and I was the maid of honor when she and Christopher married shortly after graduation. Seven years later, she was the maid of honor in my wedding.

Our friendship is deep and rich, forged in two years of shared daily life and sustained through eleven years of living in different states and pursuing different callings. She makes pottery; I write. She's been a stay-at-home mom for years; until recently, I had a teaching career. We're not the kind of friends who talk on the phone every week or even every month, but when we do see each other, there is trust and understanding and volumes of mutual care and respect.

In my own journey of motherhood, Mary Grace has always been willing to listen and pray and grieve and celebrate with me, and I know her motherhood story well too: the struggle she faced when her oldest son refused to nap for more than thirty minutes at a time, the whirlwind delivery of her second son in a hospital wheelchair, the long months she and Christopher waited to get pregnant with their third—a daughter just a few months older than Ellie.

But last fall, only months after Avaleen's death, I was taken completely by surprise when she called to tell me about her own miscarriage. I hadn't known she was pregnant, and though I don't recall us ever talking about it, I'd developed the impression that she and Christopher were finished having children. They'd thought that too, she shared over the phone, but she'd gotten pregnant unexpectedly and then, within a matter of weeks, miscarried. It was complex, she said, to try to embrace a life you weren't planning for and then, still reeling from that news, have to let that life go. Deep in my own grief, I mourned with her. Our situations were different, but it was easy to understand each other. We were both mothers missing our babies.

Ellie and I arrive at the Peters's Lancaster City home, located a few blocks from where my parents live, late on a sunny Wednesday afternoon. My energetic two year old has fallen asleep in the car, and I have to wake her up to carry her in. We find the Peters in the process of waking up too. Hannah, also age two, is fresh from a nap as well, and Caleb and Jonathan, seven and five, have just returned from school. Mary Grace and I chat easily while Hannah and Ellie stare at each other, unfamiliar, wary.

Eventually, the kids find their way to the long wooden dining room table and a large bin of Play-Doh. I ease my pregnant body onto a seat beside Ellie, and Mary Grace stands at her kitchen counter facing us, chopping the vegetables she's planning to roast for dinner and whipping up a batch of chocolate cupcakes for dessert. Light shines bright through a row of large windows adjacent to the table. An hour passes, filled with busy little voices, before Christopher arrives, and we clean up the Play-Doh and sit down for dinner.

After homemade spaghetti sauce and cupcakes decorated with pink sprinkles shaped like tiny pigs, we get all four kids tucked into bed, leave the dishes piled in the sink, and head to the living room. It's comfortable, the three of us; we've sat together like this on many nights in the years before CJ came along. I grab a chair, and Christopher and Mary Grace stretch out on opposite ends of their olive green corduroy couch. It's a sofa bed they purchased when they first got married, and I remember sleeping on it whenever I visited their various Raleigh, North Carolina apartments. Back then, we never dreamed we'd be sitting here, five living children between us, talking about the babies we've lost.

I ask them to begin by telling me their stories of faith. I think I know them well, I say, but I want to be sure.

Christopher goes first, recounting a childhood similar to my own: Christian home, regular church attendance, a commitment to follow Jesus as a child of five. "It was never not a part of my life," he says. "It's kind of straightforward."

Mary Grace also grew up in a Christian home, attended church regularly as a child, and made an early profession of faith, but her teenage years were more tumultuous. Her mother's battle with bipolar disorder left her hurt and confused, and in high school, she says, "I did go through a period of questioning and kind of went off the deep end for awhile."

During this time, she attended a Phish concert with some friends and tried acid for the first and only time. She explains, "God used the hallucinating properties there to kind of smack me upside the head and show me just what life would be like if I did not have Him in my life. I remember distinctly coming out of that . . . feeling a complete void."

After this experience, Mary Grace began the process of turning back to God and asking Him to heal the wounds of her childhood, a journey that continued into college. Both she and Christopher were involved in the Navigators campus ministry and served together on the worship team, Mary Grace on *djembe* drums, Christopher on piano.

"What would you say drew you to each other in that time?" I ask, trying to remember exactly how it all started.

"That bump on the other side of the keyboard," Mary Grace laughs. "It was just a bump of a head."

Christopher is more matter of fact. "She was a great woman of God, and she was able to disciple and pass that along to other women, which I valued."

"There's a steadiness about him," Mary Grace says, more serious now. "What you see is what you get."

I smile. They are quite different, these two. Christopher is structured; Mary Grace is spontaneous. He loves details; she forgets to eat lunch most days. He's an architect; she's a potter. I've watched them wear at each other's edges over the years, their differences sometimes grating, but they've become better for it, their marriage smoother, more cohesive. They're a good team.

"What were your expectations and desires for having a family when you got married?" I ask.

"I wanted to have five kids," Christopher says. "Four or five."

"I did not like being an only child," Mary Grace adds. Having grown up admiring the family of her mother's sister, in which there were four children, she explains, "I always thought four would be the perfect number."

Christopher and Mary Grace waited two and a half years after their marriage to start trying for a child and learned they were pregnant with Caleb around the time of their third anniversary. Fourteen months after Caleb's birth, they decided to try for another baby and got pregnant with Jonathan almost immediately. The boys are twenty-three months apart.

Things didn't progress as quickly the third time around. It took nine months for Christopher and Mary Grace to get pregnant with Hannah, nine months that overlapped almost exactly with the first nine months CJ and I began trying to get pregnant ourselves. I remember talking to Mary Grace during that time and how careful she was to avoid making much of their difficulties, how aware she was of the blessing of her two healthy boys and of the depths of my concern that I might never be able to have children. But I knew it was a hard time for her.

"I hated the cycle," she says. "You're a couple days late, and you get really excited. It's like going up a roller coaster, and then it's just like the bottom falls out."

Both she and Christopher are quick to acknowledge that those months were only a small taste of infertility, not in the same category as the much longer and more complicated journeys they've walked with other friends. From my current vantage point, I feel much the same way. I tasted the pain of infertility in the year before Ellie was conceived, but I know only hints of what it feels like for those who've known that ache year after year.

"It was long enough," Mary Grace says, "that I was starting to work through . . . really letting God move and trusting Him with whatever the outcome . . . but I really felt like I was just touching on a very significant journey that other people have."

It took nine months, but God answered Christopher and Mary Grace's prayers for a child and Caleb's prayers for a baby sister and gave them Hannah. Shortly after her arrival, both Christopher and Mary Grace began to feel like their family might be complete.

"I remember bringing her home from the hospital," Mary Grace says. "We both had this full feeling . . . a contentedness with the number of people here in our family."

"Yeah," Christopher elaborates. "We can take this and move on to the next stage of life . . . We can get out of the nights awake and the diapers and we can move forward with this. We did feel that way."

My back aches from a day full of sitting, so I shift my body down onto the floor.

The Peters say they continued to discuss the possibility of more children from time to time, but they remained uncertain. Then, in October of 2012, with Hannah nearly two, Mary Grace realized her period was unusually late. After two pregnancy tests and two positive results, she and Christopher were forced to face the fact that she was six weeks pregnant.

"I remember feeling heavy," Mary Grace says.

"Reeling was a good word," Christopher adds. "I think I was in shock."

"It's strange," Mary Grace continues. "With the other ones . . . the months of waiting or wanting made that moment of seeing the positive on the stick joyous and exciting and a celebration. This time it was just kind of like—" She stops and takes a deep breath.

"Yeah," Christopher says. "All the camping trips and whatever else we thought we were going to do were all gone, instantly put on hold."

Mary Grace felt particularly overwhelmed at the thought of another child to care for. She remembers one evening, the news of her fourth pregnancy still fresh, when she realized dinner needed to be ready early because the boys had soccer practice that night. Christopher was due home any minute, and she hadn't even started cooking. It had already been a particularly challenging day with the kids, and in that moment, she lost it. "I could not hold it together any longer," she says. "I was sitting on the kitchen floor just sobbing, and he came home from work, and the kids were bouncing off the walls."

The tears came, she says, because she felt both incapable of taking on the burden of another child and guilty for not being excited about a new baby. "*I don't want this*," she says, describing her thoughts at the time, "*but I don't want to not want it*. It's a life and it's a gift . . . but emotionally, I'm just in this place of, *What have we done?*"

She and Christopher told two other couples their news, but for the most part they kept it to themselves. They didn't know how to share their confusion, particularly with those who longed for children themselves. "*How can I go back to my life group*," Mary Grace recalls wondering, "*and say, 'I'm pregnant with my fourth child and I'm struggling with it,' when here's this woman across the room from me who's had two miscarriages and has been trying to have kids for five years?"*

I nod. Having been the woman struggling with infertility and the woman grieving the death of a baby, I know that it might have been difficult for me to respond graciously toward someone in Mary Grace's position. I think back to last month's interview with Cathy and recall how challenging it was for her to sympathize with her friend during an unwanted pregnancy when she so desperately wanted to be pregnant herself. I wonder how I would have reacted if Mary Grace had chosen to call me with her news. *Would I have been able to set aside my own grief at the loss of Avaleen months earlier and care for her as she tried to accept a pregnancy she didn't plan for? Would I have been able to see what I believe to be true, that attempting to judge pain on some type of comparative scale is an unhelpful exercise?* I hope so, but I'm not sure.

Sitting with them in the living room, though, I *do* feel bad for Christopher and Mary Grace. I hate that they had to face their burden alone. I don't know what it's like to experience an unplanned pregnancy. My first reaction to the sign of a positive pregnancy test has always been happiness. But I also know, after three pregnancies and two years of parenting, that having a child is a huge sacrifice, daunting even when it's an answer to long-held desires and many months of prayer. I recognize there is a very real struggle when you realize you are being called to a sacrifice you weren't prepared for, one you didn't ask for or choose.

While Christopher and Mary Grace tried to process the reality of another baby on the way, Mary Grace says she noticed almost immediately that this pregnancy was different from her others. She didn't have any of the secondary characteristics she'd experienced early in her other pregnancies: enlarged breasts and tenderness or gagging when she brushed her teeth. The absence of these symptoms didn't strike either Christopher or Mary Grace as a cause for concern, but they do say it made the whole experience even more surreal.

"I felt like it wasn't real for some reason," Christopher muses. He recalls thinking, "*Is this a dream? Or is there an undo button here? Because it just doesn't . . . it doesn't connect with me right now.*"

He was also worried that maybe they wouldn't be as good or as loving of parents to a baby they hadn't asked for. But Mary Grace was gradually coming to peace with the idea. "In two weeks," she says, "I'd gotten to the point where I was still not loving the idea, but I wasn't terrified any longer and I wasn't reeling from it." She began to believe that "somehow God's going to give me the grace to walk through this."

Then, suddenly, at what Mary Grace calculated to be eight weeks into her pregnancy, she started to bleed. "I'd never even spotted with any of my other pregnancies," she says. "You're thinking in part, *This could be something bad.* And then on the other part, you're thinking, *Maybe this is just going to be spotting.* I really just didn't know."

The bleeding began in the evening, and she called her doctor the following morning. The doctor scheduled an ultrasound at the hospital for her that night.

It was late when she and Christopher arrived, around ten p.m. An ER tech performed the ultrasound and—unable to tell Christopher and Mary Grace anything herself—called Mary Grace's doctor, who spoke to them on the phone. The doctor told them the results of the ultrasound were inconclusive. The technician couldn't find a heartbeat, but because the baby measured at about six and a half weeks, he said, it was possible the heartbeat was simply not yet detectable.

Mary Grace knew almost immediately that scenario wasn't possible given the date of her last period. "That didn't make sense timewise," she says. "So the only feasible answer was that the baby died at six and a half weeks, and here I am at eight weeks. My body's finally processing that [baby] out."

And yet, because no one had told them definitely that their baby had died, a glimmer of hope remained, at least for Mary Grace. "The heaviness of it all didn't hit until later," she says.

They left the hospital with instructions to check in with the obstetrician the following morning. Mary Grace woke up so ill that she asked Christopher to stay home from work and take care of the kids. She was pale, nauseous, and having hot sweats. "I could not get out of bed," she says. "It literally felt like my body was trying to get rid of a piece of itself. "

I've never heard anyone describe a miscarriage in exactly this way. "Was it similar to labor at all?" I ask. I've never really been in full-blown labor either, since I had to have a C-section with Ellie, but I am curious all the same.

"It was worse," Mary Grace says immediately.

She called her doctor's office, and they asked her to come in right away. Because she didn't want to drag the kids along, she asked Christopher to stay home with them and drove herself to the office. She was so sick, however, that she couldn't even sit upright in the waiting room. "I'm white as a sheet, and I look terrible," she says. "I haven't showered. I'm just there. I laid down on this bench and thought I just wasn't going to make it."

A nurse finally called her back to an exam room, where she threw up twice. "My body's absolutely freaking out in every capacity," she recalls. "I don't remember the pain as much as the sensation . . . that something was wrong and something was trying to come out."

An internal exam revealed that Mary Grace had already begun to dilate. Her midwife asked if she wanted to go home and try to pass the baby on her own or if she'd rather go to the hospital for a procedure to remove it. Mary Grace chose the latter, but in spite of the fact that she'd just thrown up, was told she'd have to wait until later in the day since anesthesia was required, and she'd eaten breakfast that morning.

Christopher picked her up, and she went home and spent the rest of day in bed. The intensity of her physical pain lessened, and a few hours later she and Christopher dropped off their kids at a neighbor's house and returned to the hospital.

The Peters felt supernatural peace and grace upon them as they waited in triage. Eventually, after they'd completed the necessary paperwork and Mary Grace had changed into a hospital gown, she said goodbye to Christopher. As she was being wheeled into surgery, a nurse bent over and asked her, "What do you want to do with the remains?"

"Oh. *Remains*," she recalls repeating. She pauses, allowing the weight of that word to settle on us all. "There's been a death in the family." For the first time, the full reality of what was happening hit Mary Grace.

The nurse presented her with three options: dispose of the baby, release its body to a funeral home, or send the body to a shared grave one of the funeral homes in the county offered as a free service to local residents. Frustrated that she had to make this decision at the last minute without her husband, Mary Grace chose the third option. Christopher says he would have done the same.

I wish our hospital had offered us choices like these. CJ and I have often talked about how we wish Avaleen's remains hadn't had to be sent for testing and then presumably disposed of as medical waste. I know we made the best decision we knew how at the time, but if I ever have to do it again, God-forbid, I know I'll do things differently.

Feeling more aware of the situation's gravity, Mary Grace asked to speak to the doctor before the procedure began. "I said, 'If you get in there and you think there's absolutely any way possible that this baby is still alive, I do not want you to do this.'" The doctor assured her that her baby was definitely gone.

A few hours later, she walked out of the hospital feeling moderately sore but generally healthy. "It wasn't physically a big ordeal," she says, commenting that she didn't even bleed much in the days that followed. "It just felt like it got all tied up in this neat little package with a bow and much too quickly."

I recall feeling similarly. I'd gone into the hospital carrying a baby inside of me and walked out a few hours later without her. By the next day, I'd felt almost completely normal, better, in fact, than I had through much of my pregnancy. I'd actually wished I'd been confined to bed, that my physical reality matched the state of my broken heart.

For Christopher and Mary Grace, part of their sorrow was tied to their initial reaction to the pregnancy. "I immediately regretted not wanting the baby in the first place," Christopher says, "almost [thinking] that somehow the fact that I didn't want the baby caused the miscarriage."

While Mary Grace knew this wasn't rational, she found her own thoughts echoed Christopher's in this way. "I felt awful," she says. "Guilt does that."

The month of November was particularly difficult. Christopher was in the middle of a big project at work, and Mary Grace had a large pottery deadline looming. "And we had this huge, heavy grief that we didn't really know what to do with," she says.

In the middle of that month, they attended a burial for their baby, a joint service for all of the babies who'd been miscarried that month and whose parents had chosen to bury them in the group plot at the funeral home. When Christopher and Mary Grace arrived, they saw a pastor and two small caskets. "They were like little white shoe boxes with a domed top," Mary Grace says, a trace of wonder in her voice.

Christopher and Mary Grace have vivid memories of the service, especially of the other parents who attended. Mary Grace recalls one woman in particular who was wearing a wedding band but attended the service alone. "She was very stoic," she says. "It struck me . . . when I saw her . . . that this was not the first time this happened to her."

They also recall several teenagers in attendance, some white, some Hispanic. "Clearly in high school," Mary Grace says. "There was another girl who came with her boyfriend and her parents and maybe a sister, and she was crying uncontrollably." She remembers seeing a Mennonite couple there as well.

"We cried," Christopher says. "We were sad for sure, but almost feeling badly for other people, knowing that we've got three kids to go home to."

"It was terrible," Mary Grace says. "It was just terrible. There's this feeling like I just buried a child."

I feel deeply as I listen to Christopher and Mary Grace talk. I am sad for them and for the nameless men and women they've described, moved by the image of a diverse group of bereaved parents and relatives standing together to acknowledge their collective losses. This is a good thing, I know, a healing thing. I wish again that we might have had some sort of burial service for Avaleen, that her life could somehow have been shared with others, more firmly grounded in place and time.

Knowing "my baby's buried a mile that way," Mary Grace says, pointing toward the window, makes her feel more settled.

Christopher says he's not sure if it was because of the service or merely a result of passing time, but that he and Mary Grace have come to the place where they see the baby they lost as their fourth child. "Whether we were in shock to begin with or not," he explains, "that was a member of the family we won't have."

In spite of this understanding, Christopher found that for him, the grief subsided after the service. He thinks from time to time about going back to visit the burial site and feels guilty that they haven't yet done so. But his emotion passed quickly. "As a guy, I didn't feel much of that early connection to the baby," he says.

For Mary Grace, though, the grieving process has been longer and deeper. There were "times throughout the year," she explains, "when I would wake up and I would feel like there's a dark cloud over me and I emotionally couldn't get past that dark cloud. Then I would realize it was the grief keeping me in that place."

"You would randomly say, 'I miss my baby today,'" Christopher says, his voice gentle.

"I would," Mary Grace says. "'I want my baby'; 'I miss my baby.'"

Mary Grace would have been due to give birth in June, near the time of her and Christopher's anniversary, and as that date approached, she found her sadness intensifying. Coincidentally, there was a family baby shower the week of her due date. She was glad to be involved and to celebrate another new life. Still, as hard as she tried not to focus on herself, Mary Grace says, "the whole time I'm thinking, *I would've been due this week. I would be holding my baby, and I'm throwing you a shower.*"

In particular, she struggled with feelings that no one remembered the child she'd lost. "*Nobody remembers my baby except me,*" she says, describing her thoughts at the time. "*Nobody thinks about this.*"

"They knew you miscarried," Christopher clarifies, "but nobody knew the due date."

"It's not seared in their brains the way it is when you're the mom," says Mary Grace.

"I had to leave the room at one point," she remembers, "and go into the laundry room and cry for a moment."

I understand this too. My brother and sister-in-law announced their first pregnancy only a few months after we lost Avaleen, and while I was happy for them, there were painful reminders too.

As the months passed for Christopher and Mary Grace, they found themselves talking often about whether or not their family was complete. For Christopher, the miscarriage seemed to confirm that God's will was for them not to have any more children, but Mary Grace felt the opposite. "I think it kind of blew open the doors of what if we did have another one?" she says. "That wouldn't be so bad."

As time passed, however, she realized, "The desire for the baby wasn't just any baby. It was the baby I'd lost."

"So not that you wanted a fourth," Christopher explains. "You wanted *that* fourth."

"I wanted the one I buried. My little Lydia."

Though Christopher and Mary Grace don't know their baby's gender and haven't officially chosen a name, they both think of her as a girl.

"I feel pretty strongly that it's a girl," Mary Grace says. "I don't know why."

"I think we would have hoped to have another girl," Christopher adds. "And maybe that's why . . . because I feel the same way."

"I don't know," I say. I tell them about a study I read in which a psychology professor found that 70 percent of pregnant women could correctly intuit the sex of their babies.[16]

"I think about her as a *her*," Mary Grace says quietly, almost wistfully, "and I think about her as Lydia . . . little Lydia girl. I still miss her." She pauses, then continues, "She'd be two and a half months old."

16. Schroedel, "Naming the Child," 118.

"Our lives would be really different," Christopher reflects.

I'm struck, as I have been at several points throughout the evening, by how unalike their grief processes have been: his relatively short and rational, hers deeper, longer. Here too, they are dissimilar, but there is respect and tenderness. They've given each other permission to grieve in their own ways.

While Christopher's closure came through the structure of the burial service, Mary Grace says hers came later, more spontaneously, after a conversation with a friend at the pool during her boys' swim lessons. She can't remember what the friend said exactly, something about people wanting to hold onto a piece of their youth, but she walked away with a clear sense that her time of grieving was over, that she could let it go. "I haven't felt as intensely about it from that point forward," Mary Grace says.

I'm aware as she relates this experience that I've yet to have such a moment, to feel a sense that it's okay for me to release my grief. I wonder if I'll ever feel that way.

"Do you have any sense of what God was up to in this?" I ask. Outside, we hear voices, kids screaming, the sounds of a city alive at night.

"I don't have a why yet," Mary Grace says.

Christopher offers his own interpretation: "There is no why."

They talk about their increased ability to relate to others struggling with fertility issues, about a deeper awareness of the imperfections of this world and of eternity, of the ability to believe that God is good in times of suffering working its way deeper into their hearts. In the end though, the clearest answer, the one that sticks with me, is Christopher's initial response: *there is no why.*

For the Peters, there is peace, peace with God in spite of their loss, peace with their family as it is—three beautiful children here, one precious little one gone.

Days after my conversation with Christopher and Mary Grace, CJ, Ellie, and I celebrate Labor Day with CJ's parents and work on an extensive list of pre-baby home improvements. I think often of the peace Mary Grace described, a peace that feels elusive to me. As this pregnancy has progressed, my questions about God no longer feel as urgent, but they linger in the corners of my mind. My sense of mourning has abated, but instead of feeling freedom to move on, I've been worrying that my excitement about this new child is somehow a betrayal of Avaleen and of the significance of her life.

How does one move on? I'm forced to admit that I don't know, that I've not yet had the sort of freeing epiphany Mary Grace described. Instead, I begin to pray that a moment like this will come, that God will show me how and when it's time to let go.

I've been thinking this week about stories, about how God often writes the stories of our lives in ways we never would have chosen. I've been thinking about my plans and dreams for family and home and life, about how much time and energy I pour into making them become reality, about how much I struggle when, in big ways or small, my plans fall to pieces. I've been realizing that my goal in life ought not to be to make my agenda come to fruition, but rather to respond to what God brings into my life—be that motherhood, writing a book, or talking to a friend, with faithfulness and obedience, trusting that He is doing good things, both seen and unseen.

—BLOG POST, SEPTEMBER 27, 2013

Chapter 12

SEPTEMBER: JOSHUA AND BETHANY

As the days turn cooler and I enter my third trimester of pregnancy, I treasure my remaining days with Ellie—just the two of us. We take a Mommy and Me ballet class together; she twirls and spins effortlessly in her little pink tutu while I waddle my large self around the room as best I can, trying to keep up. We host weekly alphabet craft time with one of her friends, and because it's finally cool enough to be outside again, we start taking several walks a day. Sometimes she pushes a baby in her doll stroller. Sometimes I push her in the real stroller. Sometimes we both walk.

One afternoon we meander out of our court and down the sidewalk toward the adjacent elementary school. The temperature is mild and the air is comfortable, absent of summer humidity. Ellie runs beside me happily, talking excitedly about the playground.

When we arrive, she takes off, eager to climb and jump and slide, and I stand for a moment and watch, enjoying the weather and Ellie's energy and the kicks of her baby sister inside me. I reflect on the independence Ellie has recently acquired, independence that allows us to leave the house with nothing but our keys.

I think of Avaleen and how different my life would be if she were with us. I'd have pushed her here in a stroller, carrying a bag full of diapers and wipes and burp cloths. She'd be almost ten months now, likely crawling, possibly working on her first steps. She'd need to be held, prevented from eating mulch, guided up steps and down slides. There would be no time for peaceful reflection.

It's a strange place, this joy I feel at life as it is, mingled with the sorrow that lingers. God feels distant from me here, and instead of pursuing Him, my mind is filled with details about the furniture I need to sell on Craigslist and the home projects I'm eager to finish before this baby arrives. I like feeling in control and getting lots of things done, but if I stop moving long enough, I know my soul isn't at rest. I feel frustrated, wishing I could somehow be more humble, more dependent, more at peace.

Mid-month, I kiss CJ and Ellie goodbye and board a plane to Portland, Maine for a weekend visit with the Anderson family. My husband and I first met Joshua and Bethany Anderson at our church in Fairfax when they moved to the area a few months before CJ and I started dating. During our engagement, we were part of a church-related small group they led and hosted in their home.

In the short time we attended their small group, it was evident to both CJ and I that the Andersons were fun, kind, and patient—people around whom it's easy to be your authentic self. On one occasion, Bethany and I met for coffee at Starbucks, and while we'd never talked at length before, our conversation that afternoon was deep and meaningful. At the time, I was struggling with a sense of sadness I couldn't explain or shake, and she shared that she too was wrestling with sadness related to her inability to get pregnant despite years of trying. I grieved with her, knowing my own desire for children and how hard it would be for that desire to remain unfulfilled.

After CJ and I married, we attended a different small group and no longer saw the Andersons as often. We knew they'd begun to pursue adoption, and we joyfully attended a silent auction fundraiser they held in our church basement and purchased gifts for the six-year-old brother and five-year-old sister they would eventually bring home from Ethiopia.

During our own year-long battle with infertility, I paid close attention to Bethany's adoption-related updates on Facebook and often watched the Anderson family at church, trying to imagine what their life was like. *Is our infertility a sign that God wants us to adopt?* I sometimes wondered. I knew it hadn't been easy, but Joshua, Bethany, and their children seemed happy together. *Could CJ and I adopt as well? Are we those kind of people?* I wasn't sure.

It's late Friday afternoon when my plane lands in Portland. After battling pregnancy-related back pain for most of the flight, I'm glad to find Bethany, her dog Belle, and her youngest daughter, Erbeka, almost four, waiting for me outside the airport. We drive about forty-five minutes north, along wooded highways, toward the Andersons's home in a tiny town called Turner. I've been hoping for a taste of Maine's fall beauty, but most of the trees here are still green, holding on to summer.

As we drive, Bethany tells me about the house she and Joshua signed a contract on this morning, a historic home built in the 1790s and recently restored. She warns me that their current home, a rental, is already being dismantled in preparation for their move the following weekend. When we initially made these plans, we had no way of knowing my trip would fall in the week between their closing date and moving day, but Joshua and Bethany have assured me in our emails over the past few weeks that they want me to come anyway, that they're happy to talk to me in the midst of their chaos.

We stop at the home of a friend to pick up Bethany's four older children, where they've spent the afternoon playing. They've never known me well and certainly don't remember me, but they greet me warmly and ask questions about my family and about some of the children they remember from our church—their first American friends. Back at the Andersons's simple three-bedroom rental, we all congregate in the open kitchen-living area. Bethany's middle daughter, Tigist, almost ten, chops onions and peppers into neat piles while Bethany combines ingredients for dinner. Her oldest daughter, Meti, sixteen, and her two sons—Enoch, eleven, and Justice, nine—flop onto the couches to watch *Little House on the Prairie*, a show I haven't seen since my own childhood. Erbeka settles next to me at the kitchen island, wanting to see pictures of Ellie on my phone, then to show me pictures of her family's camping and beach adventures on their laptop.

There is bustle and busyness here, I note, but it's also peaceful and pleasant. I'm struck by the independence of the Anderson children, by the absence of tears and tantrums and diaper changes. This is what I've always pictured when dreaming of a large family, and I feel encouraged as I think of the future, even as I recognize CJ and I are many years away from having children this age in our home.

Later, after the rest of us have eaten dinner, Joshua returns from work and an evening of church worship team practice. The Andersons tuck their kids into bed, the three girls in one small downstairs bedroom, the boys in another, and then we sit upstairs in the box-lined living room to sip tea and talk, Belle snuggled beside us on the floor, sleeping.

It becomes evident quickly that Joshua and Bethany's stories have been intertwined almost from the beginning. They met in third grade. In fifth grade, Bethany says, Joshua once chucked erasers at her during social studies class. In middle school, Bethany, who'd grown up in a Christian home, started inviting Joshua, whose family was not religious, to attend youth group with her. Over time, they both say, Joshua and his sister became close to Bethany's entire family, and they grew to think of each other as brother and sister.

At first, Joshua attended youth group simply because it was something fun to do. "It was that or homework," he says. "There were a lot of cute girls there and . . . dodge ball, pizza."

But as time passed, the tenets of Christianity began to make sense to him. First, he began to believe there was a God; eventually, at a large youth event he attended at age fourteen or fifteen, he understood himself to be sinful and God to be holy and felt called to repentance and faith in Christ.

In their youth group, Joshua says, Bethany was known as a pioneer. In rural Northern Maine where they grew up, people didn't often leave the state; Bethany signed up for a mission trip to Panama. "Everybody, myself included, really admired her faith," Joshua says. "Being willing to step out there and do impossible things for God."

A car passes by outside, and Belle lifts her head, her collar jingling.

Joshua, on the other hand, was known as "probably the best hacky sacker," Bethany says, laughing. But she began to notice other things about him too: his tenderness and compassion, his heart to worship God.

It wasn't until fall of their senior year, however, that Bethany realized she'd begun to develop feelings for Joshua beyond friendship. They went on a church mission trip to Mexico together and started dating a few months later. "I think we actually went on one date by ourselves," Bethany laughs. "To see the movie *Life Is Beautiful*, and we got extra credit for it in our Spanish class because it was a foreign film."

While their interest in one another remained strong, they put their relationship on hold for a few years while they both participated in an internship program with a Christian organization called Teen Mania. Interns were not allowed to date one another, and when the program was over, they decided to go their separate ways: Joshua to continue working for Teen

Mania, headquartered in Texas; Bethany to pursue a degree in anthropology at University of Southern Maine.

But within a few months, they were emailing again and soon began dating long distance. The following summer, Joshua moved back to Maine, and a few months later, he proposed to Bethany over the loudspeaker on a flight to a friend's wedding. After a nine-month engagement, they were married. Then, the week after their honeymoon, they packed their few possessions into Joshua's station wagon and headed to Dallas, Texas where Joshua was to begin Bible college.

"We were living on faith," Joshua says. "And love."

"And our wedding money," Bethany laughs.

Their insurance policy only covered catastrophic events, so at first, Joshua and Bethany decided they'd wait to start trying for children. However, Bethany's body didn't handle birth control well, and after a few months, she stopped taking it. "We just said we'll trust God and see what happens," Bethany recalls.

Joshua and Bethany wanted children and expected to have three or four eventually. Because they'd both had extensive missions experience overseas, including visits to orphanages, they shared a desire to adopt at some point. However, they'd always wanted biological children first. "That was Plan A for us," Joshua says. "We thought it would be neat to adopt, but it was never Plan A."

It's getting late, I notice, and because we all plan to be up early for the kids' soccer games in the morning, we decide to stop for the night. Joshua and Bethany insist I sleep in their bed, and while I feel guilty leaving them on an air mattress in their own living room, my pregnant body is relieved.

The next day is full, as I imagine most days are in a busy family of seven. We're out of the house by eight, shivering on the sidelines and cheering loudly, first for Tigist and then for Enoch and Justice. Afterward, we eat lunch on the floor of the Andersons's new home. We take in its beauty: exposed ceiling beams, wide hardwood floor planks, sparkling new appliances, and lots of bright, warm, natural light. It's the first time the kids have seen the house, and they run from room to room with excitement, planning the layouts of their bedrooms.

Outside, there's an apple tree, a pond, and several acres of wooded land. After lunch, we go exploring. The boys swing sticks like machetes in the long grass, clearing pathways, and Bethany points out the places where she imagines a chicken coop and a garden will someday go.

Mid-afternoon, we return to the rental. I nap while the kids rest quietly in their rooms. When I come upstairs, I find Joshua and Bethany on their computers, researching pellet heaters and bamboo growth removal for their new property. The house stirs to life again, filled with running feet and happy voices, and then all eight of us pile into the van and Joshua's car. The Andersons want to take me out for a special dinner at one of Bethany's favorite restaurants, Ruby Tuesday's. They haven't been there since Mother's Day, she says, and it is not lost on me that dinner out for a family of seven is an expensive and therefore rare occurrence. The kids are well-behaved and appreciative, and when Joshua insists on paying for my meal too, I feel loved, overcome by all the good that is here in this family.

Later, once the kids are in bed, Joshua, Bethany, and I sit down again upstairs, tea in hand. We jump right back in where we left off: after over a year of marriage and a year off of birth control, when Joshua and Bethany began to wonder if something was wrong.

"That little alarm kind of went off," Joshua says. "It was like, *We probably should be seeing some kids.*"

When they reached two years without a pregnancy, Bethany asked her doctor during an annual checkup if she should be concerned. Because they were young and healthy, the doctor discouraged them from rushing into fertility testing and suggested they keep trying.

But as more months passed, Bethany began to really struggle with their inability to conceive. "We didn't really have any peers having kids," she says, "but I think . . . in my heart there was an emptiness."

At the same time, she and Joshua were studying and thinking about the doctrine of God's sovereignty, a belief that previously had not been central to their understanding of the Christian faith.

For Joshua, it was becoming increasingly clear that God "doesn't only know the future, but He actually plans the future and His plans are good."

For Bethany, however, particularly in light of their ongoing experience of infertility, this doctrine only created more internal turmoil. "I went through a time where I was really angry," she says. "I wrestled through the whole [idea that] if God is sovereign, then He wants this horrible thing for me."

She remembers pulling into the church parking lot one Sunday morning and telling Joshua she wasn't going inside. "*If God is sovereign,*" she remembers thinking, "*and He can just do whatever He wants, then I don't want to be a Christian.*"

Joshua drove her home, and she went into their bedroom where she had an experience she describes as being "totally overwhelmed with God's presence." From that point on, she believed that God was sovereign, even as she continued to wonder why He allowed her and Joshua to experience infertility.

I'm moved by this honest moment in Bethany's story. While God's sovereignty has always been a challenging doctrine for me, I've never had a breaking point like the one she describes. *But perhaps,* I think, *I should.* Bethany, like Job, poured out her questions before God, and in return, she encountered Him in a deep and profound way. Often I try to work things out in my own head, afraid that if I ask God for answers, I will hear only silence. But I want to be like Bethany. I want to approach God honestly and expectantly. I want to encounter His presence and be overwhelmed by Him.

After this experience, Bethany found herself in a new place of peace, but months continued to pass without a baby. She and Joshua relocated to Northern Virginia, and as they approached three years of infertility, they decided to pursue testing. The standard tests for each of them came back normal, and they were told that if they wanted to proceed, they'd have to undergo further tests and treatments—this round more expensive and invasive. Uncertain, the couple took some time to pray.

During this period of waiting, a friend from the Andersons's small group gave Bethany a book about infertility. As yet another childless Mother's Day neared, Bethany began to read it. She pulls out one of her journals and reads an entry from that time: "*It haunts me. I try to be brave and just shut off my heart and read the stupid book. Even now writing this, I'm tempted to stop, rip out this page, and harden my heart.*" Her voice breaks, but she continues, "*But may it not be so, and dig deeper Lord. I repent and let the cross come into view today.*"

My eyes moisten as I listen, knowing well the deep, deep longing to have children and knowing too at least a taste of the deep place of submission that is required to place those desires in God's hands.

Bethany reads on, "*The author shares, 'Most often, He seemed to answer [my prayers] with a simple, deeply probing question: Do you trust me? Do you trust me to handle the future of your family? Do you trust me to know what I'm doing with your life?'*"[17]

17. Flowers, *Infertility,* 10.

The months that followed, she says, were a journey to the place where she could answer those questions in the affirmative. "God [was] just kind of recycling that question in my heart, *Do you trust me?*"

There were many dark and difficult moments. On Mother's Day, Bethany didn't want to go to church because she couldn't bear the thought of sitting and watching all the mothers stand to be honored and receive flowers or gift cards. I nod. I remember my own difficult Mother's Day after we'd been trying to get pregnant for nearly a year.

I can also relate to the other challenging moments Bethany recalls: the pregnancy announcements of close friends and family, the baby shower invitations, the times she was certain she was pregnant and then wasn't.

"Occasionally," Joshua says, "we got the question, 'When are you guys going to have kids?' The classic."

"Yes," Bethany says, "you want to break down right there."

We can laugh about it now, all of us, but it's a laughter born from shared pain, from a time when the pain was too deep for laughter.

"How was that year for you?" I ask Joshua before taking a sip of tea.

"It's kind of a blur, really," he says. "I did struggle a little bit with being frustrated about not having kids, but also struggling to learn to care for Beth because she was in a more sensitive place."

I imagine CJ would say something similar. He was disappointed when we couldn't get pregnant, but probably found it more difficult to help me deal with my emotions than he did to manage his own.

There was another frustration Joshua remembers: "wanting to fix it but not having any ability to do so."

According to Bethany though, Joshua worked hard to stay engaged, asking her to let him know anytime she was feeling down so they could pray together, and he could help remind her of what was true. "He did very well caring for me in that time," she says.

Eventually, Bethany was able to come to what she refers to as a "place of surrender." Part of it had to do, she says, with unwrapping her identity from a vision of motherhood and realizing that she was, first and foremost, a daughter of Christ. But a lot of it came down, quite simply, to trust. "I can honestly say I just had peace that God was in control," she explains.

As her trust in God's good plan for her deepened, she and Joshua felt ready to move forward with a different approach to becoming parents. "We kind of had fertility treatment versus adoption on the table," Bethany explains. "And we said, 'If we're building a family, it's one of these two options.'"

The more they talked, the clearer their choice became. It's not the same for every family in their position, Bethany acknowledges, but for her and Joshua, they felt they couldn't justify spending their time, money, and energy on fertility treatments when they knew God had given both of them a heart for adoption years ago.

When they reached that conclusion, she says, "We dove in head first." They attended a seminar hosted by a local adoption agency and immediately began to mull over what type of adoption they would pursue. They considered domestic adoption briefly, but couldn't stop thinking about the orphans overseas who end up in forms of institutionalized care not permitted in the United States.

"We both had these burning images," Bethany says.

"We had seen it," Joshua follows.

Plus, Bethany continues, "we have such a heart for the world; we'd always kind of seen a multi-ethnic family. So we landed there [on international adoption] very quickly."

The process of choosing a country to adopt from came down to practicalities. They explain that many countries have rules about who can adopt: minimum ages or years of marriage, net worth requirements, extensive in-country stays not feasible given Joshua's limited vacation days.

"That's how practical it was," Joshua says.

"When it got down to it, we were like, 'Ethiopia works really well,'" Bethany continues, laughing.

At first, the Andersons planned to adopt an infant. But the social worker doing their home study encouraged them to fill out their paperwork more broadly, just in case they changed their minds. Then, their adoption agency sent out a list of children who were currently in the orphanage waiting to be adopted. Many of these children were older and/or had special needs. Joshua and Bethany were drawn to a photo of one particular child, a deaf boy, and inquired about the possibility of adopting him only to discover he'd already been placed with a family.

But they couldn't stop thinking about the other children on the waiting list. "I think we asked the question, 'Why would we wait when they're waiting?'" Bethany says. "And so I think in a matter of about a week, we went from an infant under twelve months to siblings under eight."

"It was pretty quick," Joshua agrees.

They filled out an application requesting two children under age eight. Bethany dropped the paperwork off at the agency on the way to her nanny job one day, and just ten minutes after arriving at work, she received a call from the agency asking if she'd like to see the referral information for a pair of siblings that met their criteria. "I remember shaking," she says.

She called Joshua, and they opened the email from the agency while on the phone together, getting their first glimpse of Enoch, age six, and his sister Tigist, age four. "It was just overwhelming . . . this picture of them together," Bethany recalls. "This sad, hard face that they both had, and Enoch had his arm around Tigist, almost in this protective way. I just melted."

The Andersons hit the ground running. They moved into a townhouse and began setting up bedrooms for their little boy and girl. They began receiving regular updates and pictures from the transition home in Ethiopia where the kids were staying. In less than six months, their paperwork was in place, and they were officially matched with Enoch and Tigist. A few months later, they were on an airplane to Addis Ababa, ready to meet their kids and bring them home.

Joshua recalls the morning they first arrived at the transition home, the day they were to meet their children. A guard in a small shack opened a silver gate to the home and allowed their car to pass through. Then, the families adopting children waited in the courtyard as the kids came out one by one. "It was kind of surreal," he says, "meeting your child for the first time."

His voice gets quiet and fills with wonder as he describes that initial meeting. "*Wow!*" he says he remembers thinking. "*You're my child. This is life-changing, world-changing. This is my first time meeting you, but I feel like I've known you.*"

He describes a picture they took at that first meeting. "I don't think our smiles could get any bigger."

Their kids spent one final night at the transition home, and then the next day, they left with Joshua and Bethany for good. Upon their return to America, Joshua and Bethany threw themselves into learning how to be parents. In many ways, Bethany says, the adjustment was similar to that of any first-time parent. Their children needed constant care as they learned English and acclimated to American culture, and she and Joshua were exhausted. At the same time, they were excited about all the firsts they were able to experience with their kids. "We didn't hear their first words," Bethany says, "but we heard their first words in English . . . We weren't there when they got their first tooth, but we were able to be there when they lost their first tooth."

Overall, things were going so well that it didn't take long before Joshua and Bethany began to consider adopting more children. In fact, ever since they'd been matched with Enoch and Tigist, Bethany had been scouring the adoption agency's monthly list of waiting children, studying the faces of kids who had yet to be placed in a home. "There was a little bit of stalking going on," Joshua says playfully.

"Your heart just goes out to these other kids who keep getting passed over," Bethany explains.

One four year-old boy in particular caught her attention, a boy she and Joshua happened to meet in an orphanage while they were in Ethiopia to pick up Enoch and Tigist. Six months after their return, Bethany couldn't get him out of her mind. "He kept tugging at my heart," she says.

With Joshua's blessing, she called the adoption agency and asked if any other families had inquired about the boy. They hadn't, but the agency told them they wouldn't be able to pursue adopting him until Enoch and Tigist had been home for at least a year. By that one year point, the boy, Justice, was still waiting for a family, and Joshua and Bethany began the process of adopting him, starting with another home study.

Knowing how in-depth and expensive the adoption process was, and also knowing they'd always wanted at least four kids, Joshua and Bethany began to think it might make sense to try to adopt a fourth child along with Justice. But their agency told them it wasn't likely to happen, as they would require the Andersons to adopt a child younger than Justice, and there were no children ready to be adopted in that age bracket. Joshua and Bethany understood, but had their home study paperwork written for multiple children just in case.

And then, Bethany saw five-month-old Erbeka on the waiting child's list. "She pulled me aside one night and had me look," Joshua says.

"I think in tears," Bethany adds.

"She was tiny and her eyes were going every which way," Joshua says. "I said, 'Well, is this possible?' I told her, 'If we can get the okay, I say we go for it.'"

Erbeka's listing indicated she was dealing with a host of medical problems, including legal blindness, failure to thrive, malnourishment, and microcephaly. The Andersons were told she was not reaching important developmental milestones like rolling over and reaching for things, and that she might never walk. Their social worker said they couldn't adopt her, that it would be too much for them to handle a baby with her medical needs while also parenting three other newly adopted children.

But the Andersons found it impossible let Erbeka go. "We couldn't get her out of our minds," says Bethany.

"Literally," adds Joshua. "We talked about her all the time."

After praying together with Bethany's parents and with their small group at church, they decided to ask again. "I know you just said no," Bethany says, recounting her conversation with the social worker. "What do we have to do?"

"We pushed and pried," Joshua continues.

One of the social worker's concerns was that the Andersons didn't qualify financially to adopt any more children. But within a matter of weeks, Joshua received a huge, unexpected raise at his job, large enough to meet their agency's requirements for adopting a fourth child.

Still, the social worker was concerned about them adopting two un-related kids, both of whom had some special needs, at the same time. She asked Joshua and Bethany a long list of questions related to how they would handle parenting four adopted children. Eventually, their answers won her over, and she said she would support them adopting both Justice and Erbeka. Her superiors at the agency required a face-to-face meeting with Joshua and Bethany, but in the end, they changed their minds too. Joshua and Bethany left that meeting with Erbeka's referral.

A few months later, they were back in Ethiopia for their court date and to meet Justice and Erbeka. Ethiopian adoption requirements had changed since their first adoptions, and now they had to make two trips to Ethiopia: one for court, then another four to six weeks later to bring the kids home.

In the time between the two trips, the Andersons knew they needed to acquire a van to transport their growing family. They only had one vehicle, a small red Neon, and they had no money to buy a larger one. They'd begun to research pricing plans and options when out of the blue, someone they knew from church called them and said he'd been praying for their adop-tions and felt God was telling him he was supposed to buy them a van. He gave the Andersons a check for ten thousand dollars.

Bethany tears up again as she recounts the story. "I go full circle. [I see] God's good plan that we could never have seen back in 2006, 2007, 2008." These are the years the Andersons struggled with infertility.

She's right, I know. In our darkest moments, we cannot see what God is doing. We cannot imagine how the pain we're feeling can be good in any way. And the truth is, we never fully know what God is up to, why we have to suffer as we do. But sometimes, like in the story of the Andersons's adoptions, we get a taste. And that taste, like this tearful moment in their living room, is sweet, because we realize the pain is mingled with the good, that sometimes the pain is part of the path to that good.

With the van purchased, the Andersons flew back to Ethiopia to bring Justice and Erbeka home. This time, the adjustment was a little more difficult, as Joshua and Bethany now had to divide their time between four children, juggling English lessons and doctor's appointments while trying to come up with a routine that worked for everyone. Even though Erbeka's vision and development progressed more quickly than they'd anticipated, she was still navigating sensory processing disorder and attachment issues.

After living in Northern Virginia as a family of six for nine months, the Andersons decided to move their family back to Maine to be closer to their extended families. At the time, they didn't have any immediate plans to grow their family further. However, shortly after their move, another local family who'd adopted from Ethiopia contacted them about some difficulties they were having with Meti, their adopted teenage daughter. Joshua and Bethany had met Meti years ago when they'd been in Ethiopia to adopt Enoch and Tigist, and they'd seen her a few times over the years. They began to pray for her in earnest and got involved in enrolling her in a residential facility in Montana for adopted children who were having trouble with attachment.

While Meti flourished at the facility, her original adoptive family decided they did not want to reunify with her. In the end, both Joshua and Bethany felt strongly that they should welcome Meti into their family. They were able to get temporary guardianship of her and bring her to live in their home. Eventually they received court-appointed legal guardianship.

"We grew to love Meti just by praying for her," Joshua says.

"It was, I think, one of the most different or unexpected additions to our family," Bethany says, "but we flew back [from Montana], and it was like we jumped into life. It's literally been one of the hugest blessings to our family."

I nod. I've seen it all weekend: Meti's ready, wide smile, the way she cares for and nurtures her siblings. I haven't seen a single pout or whine, but I've watched her snuggle Erbeka, mix up no-bake cookies to share, and help Bethany with chores around the house. I'd be delighted to have a teenage daughter like her someday.

It's been nearly two years since Meti's joined their family, not even five since Enoch and Tigist first arrived from Ethiopia. Joshua and Bethany love the family they have, but they both sense it's not yet complete. "I would say at this point we're probably not done having children or caring for children," Joshua says.

They talk from time to time about fertility treatment, and, of course, the possibility of more adoptions remains on the table. After all, though they have older children, Joshua and Bethany are only in their mid-thirties themselves.

"How has adoption redeemed your experience of infertility?" I ask. I want to know if they still consider infertility a trial, if they still long for biological children.

"It's really turned from a frustration into a curiosity," Joshua says.

Bethany adds, "I think there are still days where you wonder, *What would our kids look like?*"

"Her nose. His eyes," Joshua elaborates.

"You ask those questions," Bethany continues, "but it's not this depression or burden that it was."

"There's fruit in our marriage," Joshua says. "In our case, it just looks different, that's all."

"And the fruit are really good soccer players that we could never attain to," Bethany says. We all laugh. At eleven, Enoch is already approaching Joshua's height, and Tigist isn't far behind. Joshua explains that their biological father was over six feet tall. "They're just so much fun," he says.

As the Andersons reflect on what they've learned through their journey, Joshua explains how he sees God's hand more clearly in the details of life. "Each little turn and twist is God preparing us for something," he says. "We don't know what it is or what it looks like."

He goes on to describe how their first five years of marriage—the long, childless years—were crucial training for their present, busy reality. "Those five years of marriage really prepared us for this roller coaster," he says.

Furthermore, he continues, they both understand their own adoption as children of God more clearly. "We were on the outside," he says, "alienated . . . God has brought us. He's pulled us in. He's chosen us. He's loved us."

There is much about their experience of infertility that has been redeemed, Bethany says, but she remains grounded in the understanding that while adoption has been healing for them and, they trust, for their children, it also means each of their children has to deal with the deep and profound absence of their biological families. Adoption "doesn't erase the loss they first had to experience," she says.

"I guess redemption always comes out of loss," she continues, reflective. "Our only hope is Christ . . . It's not in becoming a mom. It's not in becoming a family. It's not in becoming a son or a daughter . . . It's not anything that you gain in this life that matters. It's your relationship with Christ."

It's a good point, I think, both as she says it and as I reflect on my time with the Andersons during the plane ride home early the next morning and in the days that follow. What I take away from their story is quite simply this: in the end, life really is about a relationship with Christ, about knowing and trusting and walking with Him, even when it is hard.

I think about Joshua and Bethany's battle to trust God when they couldn't conceive a child, about Bethany's tearful prayer that she would not harden her heart, about the beautiful family they have now, one they never could have imagined or planned for on their own. It gives me faith for my own future, for the unknowns of the next few months of life with a newborn and toddler, for the bigger questions about whether or not we'll someday add more children to our family.

God has a plan, I remind myself. *It's unlikely to be easy, but it is beautiful, and it is good.*

My brain swirls with things to do: meals I want to freeze, piles of clutter to tackle, Pinterest projects I want to make for the girls' new rooms. CJ says I'm creating projects, orders me to stop and relax and rest.

It all seems so important. I wake up each morning hardly knowing where to begin and watch my to-do list getting a bit longer each day. There are only seven weeks left, maybe fewer.

—BLOG POST, OCTOBER 16, 2013

Chapter 13

OCTOBER: ALEX AND AMANDA

I wake one morning to an email informing me that an acquaintance's sister has experienced a stillbirth at thirty-eight weeks—sudden, unexpected, and unexplained. I read the message over and over, and I keep imagining this baby's nursery, neat and ready, its emptiness now a painful reminder. I think of our own nursery, of the tiny clothes already folded into tidy rows in dresser drawers.

Later that morning, I meet some friends at a playground. The other moms all have two children, a baby and a toddler each, and then there's Ellie and me and my very pregnant stomach. It's a perfect fall day, the sky bright, leaves drifting lazily to the ground. My friends chat freely, exchanging ideas about toddler tantrums, infant sleep, and strategies for filling the long days.

I have things to say about all of these topics, but on this day I do not want to talk. Ellie wanders to a corner of the park and I follow, happy for some distance. She climbs an aging piece of playground equipment, and I stay close, making sure she doesn't slip or fall. Tears spill down my cheeks, tears I can't quite explain. I dry them with the sleeve of my sweatshirt while Ellie, oblivious, happily spins a steering wheel and scoots her way across a swinging bridge.

I'm sad for this mother I don't know, for a loss deeper than my own. At first, I think the emotion I'm experiencing is fear for my unborn child, and this is part of the truth. I am afraid. The seven weeks that remain until my due date, weeks that only yesterday seemed too short for all I wanted to fill them with, suddenly feel interminably long.

But I know it's not just fear that's making me cry. These tears, I realize, are for Avaleen. Another mother's story has reminded me again of the horror of death and of the little girl who might have been here with Ellie and me today, toddling her way through the leaves. I drive Ellie home and let the tears flow. On a different day, I will write a card to the mother who's lost her baby and send her a book I think she might find helpful. But today, I do the only thing I can: I grieve.

———

A few days later, I pack my bags for a final out-of-town trip before our baby arrives. CJ stays home with Ellie, and I drive north toward Lancaster once again. This time, I'm interviewing a family I've never met before, a couple who's related to a family friend.

It's a dreary afternoon, and as I near my destination in rural Lancaster County, rain drops begin to streak my windshield. Still, the hayfields are golden, a stark contrast against the dark grey skies. I wind my way through unfamiliar back roads and over narrow, one-lane bridges toward Alex and Amanda Robertson's farm. It's ironic that my desire to talk to a couple who's pursued IVF has brought me from one of the wealthiest, most technology-oriented counties in the nation to conservative farm country, where families are rooted to their land and change comes slowly.

When I finally arrive, it's dusk. A small boy is playing near the front porch, and I tell him hello as I walk toward the door. Inside, Amanda is just as cheerful and effervescent as she's been the few times we've spoken over the phone. Alex is a quiet contrast, polite and engaged, but happy to let his wife do the talking. They tell me the boy I saw on my way in is their son Jackson, age three.

The family lives in an old farmhouse, one that Alex says most likely dates back to the early 1800s. They've renovated much of it themselves, and it's decorated simply and tastefully, notably absent of the clutter one typically expects in a house where there are children. I join the family for dinner in their large dining room. Even with all of us gathered at one end of the table, there's room for at least another seven or eight. Too much room. Amanda apologizes for the missing trim around the door frame and the unpainted patches of drywall behind her; they haven't had the time or resources to finish remodeling with all they've been through the past few years.

"Your home is lovely," I tell her as she spreads a beautiful dinner before us; beans, rice, chicken, and homemade salsa are artfully arranged on a platter. The food is flavorful, and while we eat, Jackson wiggles in his seat while I try to get to know this family. We talk about Alex's jobs, how he splits his time between working as an auto mechanic and tending to his responsibilities around the farm. He raises pigs and chickens, he tells me, and grows corn, soybeans, and barley.

After dinner, while Alex is upstairs putting Jackson to bed, Amanda and I remain at the dining room table as she begins telling me their story. Alex joins us a few minutes later, once Jackson is quiet. Like most people in Lancaster County, Amanda says, she and Alex grew up in church-going families. Amanda made a profession of faith when she was four years old; Alex recalls dedicating his life to God as a teenager. Though neither of them were Mennonite, they met at the local private Mennonite high school.

From the start, Alex liked Amanda and Amanda's mom liked Alex, but Amanda wasn't interested. "I really tried to like him," she says, "but it was just not clicking."

She recognized, though, that he was "a really good guy," and so they continued to hang out from time to time. Eventually, after high school, Alex won her over, or as Amanda puts it, God changed her heart. They dated for a year and then got married after a seven month engagement. Amanda was twenty-three, Alex one year younger.

Amanda suggests we move to the living room, where it's more comfortable. It's dark outside now, I notice as I enter. I seat myself on a leather recliner, and Alex and Amanda choose spots next to one another on the adjacent couch. The room is dimly lit, and it's quiet, the kind of quiet one only finds when surrounded by land instead of people.

For as long as she can remember, Amanda says, she wanted to have children—and lots of them. "I was always obsessed with babies," she explains, recalling how she helped out in the church nursery starting at age five and began babysitting at seven. "They threw up, they needed their diaper changed, I didn't care. I'd do it all."

Amanda also remembers knowing early on that some people were not able to have children; she watched two of her aunts battle infertility related to endometriosis and eventually adopt. While Amanda loved her adopted cousins, she remembers feeling worried as a child about whether or not she would be able to have children of her own. "It was . . . my biggest fear," she says. "Hearing about a miscarriage or anything like that, I would just cry. It was so real to me at such a young age."

While I can relate to Amanda's deep and early desire to be a mother, I cannot relate to her childhood concerns. I grew up with awareness of my mother's miscarriage, but for some reason it didn't occur to me to worry too much about having one of my own. I guess I just assumed it wouldn't happen to me.

Alex says that he and Amanda planned on having somewhere between three and five children. "I was afraid," Amanda says, "but hopeful it would work."

"I wasn't really concerned," Alex counters. Amanda shared in earlier conversations with me that her husband is the steady to her extreme personality, and I see their temperaments emerging as they talk: her persistent worries, his stable responses. I'm reminded of CJ and the similar dynamic in our marriage.

About a year and a half after they were married, Amanda, who was in cosmetology school at the time, was talking with one of her aunts while giving her a pedicure. As they conversed, Amanda realized she was experiencing many of the same symptoms of endometriosis her aunt was describing. The aunt told Amanda she needed to see a doctor immediately. "The longer you wait," Amanda explains, "the worse off it is."

After testing, Amanda was devastated to learn she did indeed have endometriosis, a disorder in which tissue that typically lines the inside of the uterus begins to grow outside of it. Scar tissue and adhesions develop in some women, and symptoms can include not only severe pain but infertility. Amanda chose to have laparoscopic surgery to remove excess endometrial tissue before she and Alex started trying.

Pretty quickly thereafter, Amanda was pregnant. "I took a bazillion pregnancy tests," she says. "[Alex] wishes he had stock in them. And I couldn't even believe it when it was positive."

Amanda battled anxiety about losing the pregnancy throughout her first trimester and dealt with difficult nausea through the end of her second trimester. Her labor was "kind of a nightmare," she says, but still, "the coolest moment in my life was giving birth to Jackson . . . I feel like that's the closest you will ever get to God here on Earth."

She and Alex decided they'd try to get pregnant again as quickly as possible, knowing symptoms of endometriosis generally worsen with every menstrual cycle and that one of the best things someone can do to treat it is be pregnant. As a result, Amanda wanted to have her children "like popcorn," she says. "Back to back and then be done."

When Jackson was between eight and nine months old, Amanda found out she was pregnant again. Though she knew having two kids close in age would be difficult, she was delighted. "I can do this," she recalls thinking. "I can have more children."

I remember feeling the same way when I found out I was pregnant with Avaleen. Any concern about having children nineteen months apart was overshadowed by an overwhelming sense of relief that conception had come easily this time.

For Amanda, however, the joy was short-lived. One week after the positive test, she started spotting. Her doctor told her it could be implantation bleeding, but she felt certain something was wrong. When she did miscarry the baby, she was devastated, both by the loss and by the failure of her plans.

"It took forever to get pregnant again," she says, then pauses and turns toward Alex. "Was that the second time that took forever?"

"I don't remember each time," he says.

"It was like three years of hell," Amanda explains, "so the timing is really hard for us to figure out."

"Basically," Alex says, "after Jackson, you got pregnant five times and had five miscarriages."

In most cases, Alex says, the miscarriages were early in the first trimester and Amanda was able to get pregnant again within a month or two. One time it took six or eight months, perhaps longer, but neither of them can remember for certain.

"People would say, 'Well at least you can get pregnant,'" Amanda recalls. "I was like, 'That isn't helping me at all.'"

I recall a well-intentioned friend who told me something similar shortly after we lost Avaleen. I remember exactly where I was standing when she spoke: facing my stove, frying fish in a skillet for the taco dinner we were about to share with our families. I remember my physical reaction to her words, the way I was suddenly aware of my stomach feeling heavy, sinking.

I'd understood her point. It *had* been a relief to get pregnant quickly on our second attempt, especially since it had taken so long the first time. But the ability to get pregnant meant little to me then. I didn't want another baby; I wanted Avaleen.

Amanda believed her repeated losses were a sign that something was wrong, but her doctors refused to perform any testing until she'd had three miscarriages. "That drove me crazy," Amanda says, "because to me that was them saying that my other two babies weren't important."

I understand the doctors' point of view. After all, miscarriages happen frequently and aren't usually caused by serious, underlying conditions. Insurance companies generally don't want to pay for tests that may not yield any helpful results, and testing can create its own undo stress and anxiety. Despite these realities, I was glad when my doctor told me that because second trimester loss was unusual, she was ordering every test she could think of. Somehow the testing, even though it didn't end up giving us any clues as to the cause of Avaleen's death, validated both my deep sense of grief and my deep desire to prevent something similar from happening again. Had Avaleen died a few weeks earlier, my doctor probably wouldn't have ordered any tests at all, and I imagine I would have felt like Amanda did: frustrated that medical professionals didn't seem willing to do anything.

During Amanda's third pregnancy, things finally seemed to be going better. She made it past the point of her other losses—to somewhere around ten weeks gestation—and remembers the overwhelming joy she felt singing in church one Sunday, thinking about her pregnancy and allowing herself to believe she and Alex were finally going to have a second baby. Then, after the service, while she was eating lunch, she started to feel cramps. "I didn't want to go to the bathroom at all," she says, "because I just knew."

Her bleeding intensified, so the next day she and Alex went to the hospital for an ultrasound, fully expecting to learn that yet another one of their children had died. However, the technician there found a heartbeat and said the baby looked completely fine. Perhaps Amanda's bleeding had been caused by a hematoma, he suggested.

A few days later, however, Amanda went into labor and delivered the baby. "I have never bled so much in my life," she says. "It was horrific."

She told the doctor from her OB group with whom she spoke on the phone that she needed to go to the hospital, but the doctor ignored Amanda's request, insisting she'd be fine at home. When Amanda asked if she should keep the baby's body for testing, the doctor's response was clinical: they didn't want to see the body, so Amanda should flush it down the toilet. "It still kind of haunts me," Amanda says. "Instead of burying my babies, they're in my septic system. I just really can't get over that."

Later, specialists will tell her she should have kept the baby, that it was old enough to be tested and might have provided valuable information about Alex and Amanda's fertility problems. To this day, Amanda says, she refuses to see that particular doctor because of the way she handled the situation.

Now that Amanda had experienced three consecutive miscarriages, her doctors finally ordered tests, looking for a cause. They could not find anything wrong, but decided to put Amanda on progesterone supplements, hoping that would help. Instead, she miscarried for a fourth time.

"I was so frustrated," Amanda says, "because my babies kept dying, but no one would tell me why or could figure it out." Adding to her frustration, she felt alone in her grief. "I love my husband to death," she says, "but he is very cut and dry. You can't do anything about it so he doesn't need to cry about it. We just try again."

Amanda was referred to a specialist, and she and Alex underwent more tests with similarly normal results. The doctors explained that the odds of a successful pregnancy increase after testing, as the tests they perform often flush the uterus and Fallopian tubes. Alex and Amanda decided to try one more time, but once again, Amanda miscarried early in the pregnancy.

The next step for the specialists was a second laparoscopic surgery to clean out endometrial tissue and to see if they could observe anything that hadn't shown up on the previous tests. Afterward, based on stretching they saw in Amanda's ovaries, they hypothesized that perhaps some endometrial tissue had grown inside her Fallopian tubes, making it difficult for her embryos to implant in the uterus in the proper amount of time.

"That was the only thing they could come up with," Amanda says. "They weren't sure."

"Yes," Alex adds. "They said they'd seen that one other time . . . At that point, they still didn't have any concrete answers."

However, the specialists believed Alex and Amanda were good candidates for IVF because they could bypass Amanda's tubes and implant a fertilized egg directly in the uterine lining.

When they'd first started seeing the specialist, Alex says, they knew IVF was a possibility, but it wasn't one they were excited about. "It was sort of a last resort that we didn't want to have to do," he says.

"Just because there's so many grey areas," Amanda explains.

"It's expensive," Alex says. "It's painful and time-consuming. Not a whole lot nice about it except for you might get a baby."

I want to ask if they'd considered adoption, but Alex goes there before I get a chance. "We talked about adoption too," he says. "It certainly would be an option . . . [but] we weren't ready to give up on having our own yet."

Amanda worried that it might be difficult to have one biological child and one adopted child, that somehow they'd treat them differently. "I didn't want to compare my kids like that," she says. She says she knows families with a mix of adopted and biological children for whom it's worked out well, but she's not sure she could do it.

Plus, she wasn't ready to let go of her dreams of giving birth again. "I don't actually know if I'll ever be done having kids," she says.

"Yes," Alex interjects, "you will be done."

We all laugh.

Still, in spite of Alex and Amanda's longing to have more biological children, IVF was not an easy or simple choice. They worried about unused fertilized eggs being destroyed, an act that Alex says would be "basically killing babies." They worried too about the practice of preimplantation genetic testing. They didn't want any of their embryos to be discarded because of genetic or chromosomal disorders.

I nod. These are some of the main reasons CJ and I decided long ago, before we even started trying to have children, that if for some reason we couldn't get pregnant, we wouldn't pursue IVF. In that case, we told ourselves, we'd rather adopt. But listening to Alex and Amanda, I wonder: *if we were in their shoes, if we'd experienced such deep longing mingled with such great heartache, might we have changed our minds?*

Amanda sends Alex to retrieve a journal from their bedroom, a journal given to her by her best friend Ruth during this difficult time. Amanda absolutely hates writing, she says, but Ruth felt it was important for her to write down her story, so for a brief time, she tried.

Alex returns with the journal, and Amanda reads a verse from it, a verse that became significant to her when she and Alex were considering whether or not to pursue IVF. The verse is I Cor 3:6–7 (NLT): *I planted the seed in your hearts, and Apollos watered it, but it was God who made it grow. It's not important who does the planting, or who does the watering. What's important is that God makes the seed grow.*

"This is how I felt God was talking to me about IVF," Amanda says, explaining that she thought of the doctor as the seed planter and the IVF hormones and medications as the watering.

Amanda knows, she says, that this passage was not written with IVF in mind. Paul, the author of I Corinthians, was referring to the seed of faith, challenging the Corinthians to stop squabbling about which church leader was better and to think of themselves as followers of God, not of particular individuals.

But as she and Alex considered IVF, Amanda had been praying that God would give them guidance. One day, after praying specifically for a sign, she came across the 1 Corinthians passage and immediately saw the parallels. I see them too. Whether conception occurs in the womb or in a test tube, God is the author of life. We now have the technology to bring egg and sperm together outside of a mother's body, but we cannot simply build a baby on our own. God must make it grow.

In the end, Alex and Amanda decided to pursue IVF, but to do so in what they believed was the most moral and ethical way possible: by making a commitment not to destroy any of their fertilized eggs and by choosing not to have their eggs tested for abnormalities.

Amanda had multiple eggs harvested and fertilized. She and Alex wanted to receive what's referred to as a fresh transfer, in which a fertilized egg is implanted without ever having to be frozen. However, after the retrieval process, Amanda experienced ovarian hyperstimulation, a syndrome that can occur when the hormones given during IVF to stimulate egg production in the ovaries cause fluid build-up in the abdomen, among other symptoms.

As a result, all of Amanda's fertilized eggs had to be frozen while she waited for her symptoms to dissipate. Two months later, doctors were able to implant one fertilized egg in Amanda's uterus. Ten days later, a pregnancy test confirmed that Amanda was, in fact, pregnant. However, within a week or so, doctors expressed concerns that Amanda's hCG levels weren't increasing at the expected rate.

During Amanda's previous two pregnancies, a similar problem had occurred. Instead of Amanda's hCG levels rising as they should have, the increase would slowly taper off until it eventually stopped altogether.

Alex and Amanda and their doctors feared this pregnancy would end the way her others had—in miscarriage.

By six weeks into the pregnancy, when the embryo was large enough to be detected by an ultrasound machine, doctors told Alex and Amanda that their baby was measuring one week behind its expected development. Often, when this happens, doctors assume a couple has their dates wrong, that ovulation and conception simply happened later than they thought. But, in IVF cases like Alex and Amanda's, the doctors knew exactly when the implantation occurred. They couldn't explain why the baby wasn't growing as it should, but they did tell Alex and Amanda that cases like these usually did not end well. They expected Amanda would miscarry within the week. "So, I'm just waiting for it to happen," Amanda says.

Strangely, the baby continued to grow, even as each week it fell further and further behind the expected measurements. Amanda made daily trips to the fertility clinic for ultrasounds and blood work, an hour and fifteen minute drive each way with Jackson in tow. Doctors continued to tell her she would miscarry, but by thirteen weeks, when patients are normally discharged from the fertility clinic and placed under the care of an OB, the baby was still alive.

The doctors at the fertility clinic were mystified. Every case like this they'd seen before had ended in death, but if the baby continued to grow, they told Alex and Amanda, they didn't see why it couldn't live. "They had a little bit of hope," Amanda says, "but they were pretty sure it was going to end in demise."

At Amanda's first visit with her OB, the doctor struggled to find a heartbeat. When she finally located one, she told Amanda to return for regular heartbeat checks. Finally, at fifteen weeks, the doctor was able to find a heartbeat easily—a good, strong one. Until this point, her doctor had warned Amanda not to get excited about a pregnancy that seemed tenuous, but on that day, the doctor felt confident. "You can get excited now," she told Amanda.

Because of Amanda's history of pregnancy loss, the doctor sent her to the hospital for an ultrasound, telling her that she and Alex could even learn their baby's gender that day if they wanted. "[The] five minutes," Amanda says, "[on] the trip from my doctor's office to the ultrasound place . . . was the only time I left myself go." She called Alex, asking him whether or not he wanted to find out the baby's gender, and she made plans to pick up a baby swing she'd seen on Craigslist after the appointment.

The excitement was short-lived. During the ultrasound, Amanda remembers the doctor not saying much, looking closely at what he was seeing on the screen. Then, he asked Alex and Amanda if they had an Amish or Mennonite background or if they were related. When they answered no to both questions, he asked if dwarfism ran in either of their families. Again, they said no. He told them he'd be back and left the room.

At this point, Amanda says she was "freaking out." When the doctor returned, his prognosis was grim. He told Alex and Amanda there was a 99.9 percent chance their baby would die. "I'm sorry," Amanda recalls him saying, "but your baby will not make it."

Amanda can't recall much else from that conversation. The baby "was measuring three weeks behind at that point," Alex says. "Simply, they'd never seen a baby that far behind make it."

Amanda wanted to know when she would miscarry. The doctor said they couldn't be sure, but it could be within the next week or two. He didn't expect Amanda to carry the pregnancy to term, but he did say that she might have a stillbirth.

"They expected the growth to quit completely and the heartbeat to stop at some point," Alex says. "Things would just tail off."

After the appointment, Amanda had to call the couple with the baby swing she was supposed to pick up. When she told the man who answered the phone that she no longer needed the swing, she lost it. "He didn't know what to say," Amanda recalls. "And I was sobbing."

Later, she received a text message from the man's wife. She told Amanda she was sorry about her news. She too had experienced a miscarriage, she said, and she was going to keep the swing for her, just in case.

Amanda was scheduled for weekly doctor's appointments, alternating between her OB's office and the maternal-fetal medicine specialist at the hospital. She received regular ultrasounds, and at around twenty weeks, she and Alex learned their baby was a girl. They watched as her growth slowed, falling to four weeks behind. Then, inexplicably, she began to hold her ground, remaining steady at four weeks behind instead of continuing to decline. "There was never a real black and white problem," Alex says, "but there [were] several things they thought could be it."

The maternal-fetal medicine doctor sent Alex and Amanda to the Children's Hospital of Philadelphia (CHOP), a world-renowned facility, for a second opinion. After a long day of rigorous testing, Alex and Amanda sat down with a team of professionals. "Their prognosis was the worst of any so far," Alex explains.

The doctors expressed concern that the baby's brain was completely smooth and undeveloped. They told Alex and Amanda there was only a 1 percent chance their daughter would be born alive, and that if somehow she was, she would have a severe intellectual disability and would eventually succumb to repeated, horrific seizures. Most likely, they said, she would die in the womb sometime within two or three weeks.

"They said I would not make it past thirty weeks," Amanda says.

Alex and Amanda left the hospital that evening, trying to prepare themselves for what now seemed imminent. After spending the day with Amanda's best friend Ruth, Jackson was home for the night, asleep, under the care of Alex's mom. Throughout Amanda's pregnancy, Ruth had come to several doctor's appointments with her, and when she didn't, she always asked Amanda to call her with an update. If Amanda didn't call, Ruth knew the appointment hadn't gone well and that Amanda needed some time to process the bad news on her own. In that case, Ruth called Amanda the morning after to find out what the doctors had said.

Amanda spoke with Ruth between appointments at CHOP to make arrangements for Alex's mom to pick up Jackson, but she didn't call with an update on their way home. She was surprised not to hear from Ruth the next morning. She remembers standing outside, sweeping the porch as she talked to Alex. "I told him I felt like I was so low," she recalls. "I'm a pretty happy person for the most part, but everything just got to me. I couldn't understand why God wouldn't let us have more children, why He would allow me to be pregnant but not be able to mother [the babies]. I told him I can't do this anymore . . . I just can't."

She went inside to get herself a tissue and heard the phone ring. She picked it up, expecting to hear Ruth's voice, but it was Ruth's husband. Something was wrong with Ruth, he told Amanda. He was at work, driving his truck several hours from home. Unable to check on her himself, he asked Amanda to go instead.

"I was picturing [that] she fell down the steps and broke her leg," Amanda says. "A real funny story."

When she pulled up to Ruth's house a few minutes later, she was surprised to see an ambulance in the driveway. Inside, one of Ruth's other friends told Amanda that she thought Ruth was gone.

"I was like, 'Where? Someone's taken her?'" Amanda says. "I did not understand."

Paramedics delivered the news. In spite of their efforts to resuscitate her, Ruth was dead.

"I just kept saying, 'Are you sure? Are you sure?'" Amanda recalls. "I remember shaking."

Amanda called Ruth's husband. Then she went to see Ruth's body, surrounded by the toys her three young children had been playing with while they tried to wake her. Amanda held Ruth's nine-month-old baby and gave her the first bottle she'd ever taken.

Amanda's voice breaks often as she tells me about Ruth, her comments occasionally trailing off into tears. "Sorry I'm so emotional," she says at one point, "but tomorrow marks a year of her death."

"Oh my goodness, I'm sorry," I say, feeling terrible that we've scheduled our interview in conjunction with such a difficult milestone. I'm still trying to take in all of this, to somehow feel the magnitude of so much tragedy in such a short time. In less than twenty-four hours, Amanda had been told by some of the top doctors in the nation that the baby inside her would surely die, and then she'd seen the lifeless body of her best friend, the woman who'd been in many ways her greatest emotional support throughout the deep suffering of the past four years. I marvel that Amanda managed not only to keep standing but to turn her energy toward caring for her friend's baby.

Just two weeks before Ruth's death, Ruth had asked Amanda to promise that she'd watch over her children if anything ever happened. Amanda had agreed and asked Ruth to do the same for her. On the day Ruth died, Amanda immediately recalled that conversation. As she sat rocking Ruth's baby, Ruth's sister, who knew of their promises, told Amanda, "Do you realize that you are both holding up your ends of the bargain? You're here holding and taking care of her babies, and she's in heaven taking care of all yours. And she's waiting for this one," referring to the baby Amanda was carrying.

"For some reason," Amanda says, "knowing that she was waiting for her helped a little bit, eased the pain."

Still, Amanda's grief was deep and intense. She wasn't really eating and was terrified to sleep. She began having lots of contractions. She'd spend hours making Alex's favorite foods, just in case he might wake up and find her gone. "I was really afraid," she says.

She pulls out her journal again, explaining that she used the book to make plans for her daughter's funeral. Instead, some of the songs and verses she'd listed were used for Ruth's service, and Alex and Amanda decided they no longer wanted a funeral for their daughter. They planned to have her cremated and to bury her ashes in a grove of trees on their property in a small, private ceremony. "I just couldn't go through all that again," Amanda explains.

Throughout grieving Ruth's death and fulfilling her promise by helping Ruth's husband adjust to caring for three children on his own, Amanda's pregnancy continued to progress. A week after their visit to CHOP, Alex and Amanda had a follow-up appointment with their maternal-fetal medicine doctor. He'd reviewed the report from CHOP and felt the doctors there painted a grimmer picture than was necessary. "He wasn't as negative that time," Alex says, while at the same time conceding, "It still wasn't good."

Against all odds, Amanda reached the thirty-first week of her pregnancy, a milestone she says "was kind of cool, I'm not going to lie."

By now, the baby was finally big enough that if she were born alive, doctors had equipment they could use to help her breathe. The Robertsons were also told that some of the concerns doctors had previously expressed about her brain no longer appeared to be such a problem. "Things looked more promising," Alex says.

Amanda is quick to clarify. "My understanding was that I might get to hold my baby alive."

In fact, around this time, Amanda's OBGYN—whom she loved dearly and who had been a great comfort to her during her miscarriages and throughout this pregnancy—took her aside. "She grabbed me real close to my face," Amanda recalls.

She said, "Amanda, you will not take this baby home from the hospital. I need you to understand that. I need you to grasp this. I know you're holding out hope that this baby will live against all the odds, but I've seen all the charting . . . and it's not going to happen . . . I want more than anything to give you a baby, but it's not going to be this one."

At thirty-four weeks, Amanda's doctors scheduled her for an induction two and half weeks later. They believed that by that time, the baby would be able to grow better outside the womb than inside it. Plus, Amanda says, "they wanted to prevent me from having a stillborn."

Amanda's thirty-five week checkup was scheduled at the hospital. She invited her mom to come with her, wanting to show her that she was in good hands and also because she was aware this might be the last chance her mom would have to see the baby alive. Together, they toured the hospital and the NICU ("just in case" Amanda explains). While Amanda was undergoing a nonstress test, her water broke.

After twenty-four hours of labor, the baby's heart rate began to drop. Doctors told Alex and Amanda their child was in distress and that they'd need to perform a C-section. Amanda had wanted to avoid surgery so she could spend as much time as possible with her baby before the little girl died, but there was no other option.

Alex was unable to join her in operating room because he passes out easily at the sight of blood. "It was really hard for me," Amanda recalls. "I wanted my rock." She also feared that if Alex wasn't in the delivery room, he'd miss his only chance to see their baby alive. Still, she was thankful her mom was present and that she could accompany her instead.

As she was wheeled into the operating room, Amanda remembers announcing, "The life of the party has finally arrived, and she's super emotional!" before bursting into tears. Her OB, who'd been up all night working, returned to the hospital to hold Amanda's hand during the procedure, and while another doctor performed the C-section, the anesthesiologist kept wiping the tears that wouldn't stop running down Amanda's cheeks. "It's going to be okay," he told her. "We're going to try and let you have as much time with the baby as we can."

Amanda remembers feeling her baby being pulled from her stomach and then hearing her scream. "For a three pound baby, that girl had some lungs," she says. "It was just the most awesome sound I'd ever heard."

At that point, Amanda couldn't see her daughter or anything that was happening, but her obstetrician came over and told her, "She's beautiful. Give or take a few toes. But she's beautiful."

"For a split second," Amanda says, "I was like, *Thank you God; this is my miracle.*"

But the doctor continued, "We'll just have to see what her MRI shows to know how long you'll get to keep her."

"So right then again," Amanda says, "I was in my doubting mode."

Miraculously, even though she only weighed three pounds, nine ounces, the little girl they named Lexington Grace only needed a small amount of oxygen and an IV for low blood-sugar while she was being cleaned after birth. "Other than that," Amanda says, "she needed nothing."

Amanda had one brief moment with Lexington in the operating room. Someone held her up for Amanda to see, and she reached out and grabbed Amanda's finger. Then, while Amanda was recovering from her C-section, doctors took Lexington to meet Alex before delivering her to the NICU.

While Amanda understood their time with Lexington would likely be short, Alex, who'd been more positive throughout the pregnancy, wasn't surprised to see his daughter alive and healthy. "Because [the doctors] were never conclusive about anything," he says, "I always thought there was a possibility she would be fine."

"What did you feel when you met her?" I ask.

"I don't know that I had any real profound feelings," Alex says. "She's just like a miniature baby."

Amanda and I laugh loudly while Alex smiles. "Oh, husband," she says fondly.

While Alex spent time bonding with Lexington, Amanda was desperate to join them. "All I wanted to do was get down there," Amanda says. "I just wanted to spend that time with her."

I can only imagine. Ellie was delivered via C-section, and I remember the long minutes I had to wait until I could hold her. If I'd been told she was to die at any moment, I would have been frantic watching her wheeled away without me.

Thankfully, Lexington did well in the NICU, and Amanda was eventually able to spend time with her there. She panicked every time she heard a Code Blue called over the hospital intercom or was told that Lexington had a rough night. "They took really good care of me in there and reassured me," she says, "but Satan still kept trying to put that doubt in my mind."

Based on what she'd been told by doctors throughout her pregnancy, Amanda continued to believe that Lexington wouldn't leave the hospital alive, in spite of her progress. One day, however, one of the NICU doctors started talking to Amanda about taking Lexington home. "I'm just looking at him blank[ly]," she recalls. She told him how she'd been warned she wouldn't ever bring Lexington home. He put his arms on her shoulders. "I'm happy to be the one to tell you," he said. "You'll be taking your baby home from the hospital."

As that doctor promised, nineteen days after her birth, Lexington came home. "I still can't believe that we got our miracle," Amanda says, looking down at ten-month old Lexington, who's spent most of the evening babbling and wiggling but is finally fast asleep in her mommy's arms.

"They've done a fair amount of follow-up testing," Alex says, "and still have no clue why or what." Except for her webbed toes and a hole in her heart that's already closed on its own, Lexington is a perfectly healthy child.

The woman who'd held the infant swing for Alex and Amanda refused to let them pay her for the swing or for any of the baby clothes she'd collected and washed for them. "Being able to be part of a miracle," she told them, "is payment in full."

All of Lexington's doctors referred to her as a miracle as well. Even Amanda's obstetrician, who is not religious, told Amanda, "I feel really good. I've never been part of a miracle before." Because of Lexington's story, she says she now believes in God.

For Alex and Amanda, their miracle baby is a source of much happiness. "I'm so overjoyed that Lexington is here and that she's alive and doing wonderful," Amanda says.

And yet, she explains, that miracle doesn't erase the hurt and the questions related to all of the suffering they've endured. "I feel like people are looking at me like there's no reason for you to be sad. You totally got your miracle," she says. "But at the same time, I didn't [get miracles] for five times. I feel like I still have so many scars."

Earlier in the evening, Amanda handed me one of Lexington's birth announcements from a pile in the dining room. I took in the angelic photos of a newborn with rosy cheeks snuggled in the arms of her mother, her father, and her adoring big brother. Except for the information about her size at birth (three pounds, nine ounces and sixteen and a half inches tall) and the phrase *prayers answered* written in script across the front, there's nothing about it that seems out of the ordinary. But Amanda's words as she handed the card to me were haunting: "The announcements are still here," she explained, "because I was too scared to send them out. I'm only now beginning to allow myself to believe she's here to stay."

Not only has Alex and Amanda's journey been far from easy, they'd still like to have more children—a possibility that's full of fearful unknowns. "I don't know if you get miracles back to back," Amanda says. "I don't know if it works like that."

"Going forward does concern me," Alex agrees.

The Robertsons are committed to implanting all of their fertilized embryos, and sometimes, Amanda worries she might suffer an untimely death before they can use them all. In that circumstance, she wonders if Alex would remarry and if his second wife would be willing to carry her babies. "Nothing can happen to either of us until our babies are taken care of," she says.

This is an anxiety I've never considered before, the burden of responsibility for embryos yet to be implanted. It's a weight I know I wouldn't want to carry.

Amanda sometimes wrestles with anger toward God about the reality of their circumstances. "I get angry at God because I do love Him so much," she says. "It's like your best friend who knows you inside and out and knows things closest to your heart and uses that against you. I feel betrayed."

Despite this, she says, she's aware of God's presence in her suffering. "It's very true what they say," she says. "In your lowest of lows, you find God. I would cry out in desperation to Him, and He would give me Scripture. It was a direct communication that I didn't ever feel in my life before."

Alex says he too has relied on Scripture to sustain him in the difficult moments. He refers to I Cor 13:12: *For now we see in a mirror dimly, but then face to face. Now I know in part; then I shall know fully, even as I have been fully known.*

"I really don't expect that we will know until we get to heaven [answers to] many of the questions we do have," he says, folding a pillow over on itself in his lap. "I guess I'm okay with that." He goes on to reference Job's famous words from Job 1:21b, the same words that came to my mind when my doctor told me Avaleen was gone: *The Lord gave, and the Lord has taken away; blessed be the name of the Lord.*

"I don't like that verse," Amanda says.

"That's not an easy one," Alex concedes, "but I do think that has been my attitude through it."

"Which is hard as a wife," Amanda says, "because I know that's your attitude . . . Not that it's wrong, it's just hard to deal with."

"Some people find experiences of suffering good for their marriages," Alex says. "I don't think we could say it's been good for us."

"We'd rather work on our house," Amanda admits.

"It wasn't detrimental," Alex clarifies. "I wouldn't say it was a positive thing."

It's getting late, and we wrap up for the night. There's no neat ending to this story, a story that's very much in process. Alex and Amanda continue to sort through their difficult past and its impact on their marriage and their faith, even as they consider the possibility of future children and the all-too-real possibility of more hurt and disappointment.

I think of them as I drive home the next morning, the lofty peaks of the Mormon Temple in view as I round the familiar curves of the DC beltway. I'm listening to Christian radio, to a song I've never heard before. I can't remember any of the particulars, but it's a song about God and the way He builds His kingdom, the sort of song that's supposed to inspire believers to march forth and do great things for God. I generally like songs like this and enjoy feeling inspired by grand visions and lofty missions.

But today, Alex and Amanda's story weighs on me. I think of them and the other families I've talked to this year. I catalogue the collective pain of their stories: decades of waiting for babies who didn't come, dozens of babies lost, lifetimes of hurt and struggle and lingering questions and doubts. I think of all the things these people might have done for God if they hadn't had to spend so much of their time wading through grief, and I try to reconcile the reality of their lives with God's call for His followers to reach others with the good news of His great salvation.

It doesn't make much sense to me. *Why would God allow His children—the people He's appointed to spread His message—to languish for years in various trials, to wrestle deeply with the very truths He supposedly wants them to share with others? Wouldn't good news be shared best and most efficiently through the strong and healthy, through people who can sing peppy songs and march forward without unresolved questions about why their babies had to die?*

In what feels like an answer, the Biblical story of Naomi comes to mind, the same story Sara Brode referenced in our interview months ago. It's an account of a woman who lost her husband and both of her children and journeyed back to her homeland far from an exemplary spokeswoman for God's kingdom. *Do not call me Naomi,* she says in Ruth 1:20, speaking to those she meets upon returning. *Call me Mara, for the Almighty has dealt very bitterly with me.*

But I know, in spite of her difficult story and the resulting bitterness, God worked both in her lifetime (to bring her joy again in the form of a grandson) and after her death (to bring *the* Savior through the bloodline of that grandson and include her story in the greatest book of all time). Her life, messy and broken as it was, became part of the advance of God's kingdom in ways she couldn't have ever imagined, even on her death bed.

As Alex said the night before, we see only in part. God alone sees the full story. He writes it. And He's very comfortable, I realize, not only with our sin, but also with our suffering selves, with the wounds we carry.

He advances His kingdom not by leading a parade of the triumphant and mighty, but by carrying in His capable arms the injured and limping, those of us who sometimes can manage nothing more than to weakly call on his name.

As the birth of this baby draws near, I find myself reflecting often on what it means to be a mother of three, to hold my love and care for three different little ones in balance. I think of Ellie and of all the changes coming her way, of the attention she will lose and the joy she will gain . . . I think of Avaleen, who'd have been celebrating her first birthday this week, and of how different our lives would be if she were here, if we'd had the privilege of knowing her.

And I think of this new baby, of what feels like an incredibly long road to her birth. I think of loss and doctors' visits and tests and waiting and nine months of fear and anticipation and anxiety. I think of the moment I will hear her first cry, and I pray it will be a sweet, redemptive moment, that in meeting her, some of the pain of losing her sister will be healed. But I know too that she is her own person, and I pray that we will be able to see her that way, that her life will be defined by the unique person she was made to be, not by the sister who was lost before her.

—BLOG POST, NOVEMBER 24, 2013

Chapter 14

NOVEMBER: JIM AND SUE

I make a simple calendar to help Ellie count down the weeks to Baby Sister's arrival: construction paper numbers strung on twine across the bay window in our kitchen. As we enter November, the days colder and shorter, only four numbers remain.

I remembered the third trimester of my pregnancy with Ellie fondly, a peaceful time absent of nausea and full of building excitement, but this time, with a toddler in tow, I feel increasingly tired. When I finally sit down each evening, my hips are sore, my ankles large and puffy.

Part of me is ready to meet my baby girl. From the beginning of this pregnancy, I've longed for the moment of finally being at the hospital, attached to heart-rate monitors and surrounded by medical professionals, people who can intervene if something goes wrong. I hate that Avaleen died without us even knowing, without a chance for us to put up a fight. Somehow, irrationally, I feel like if we'd only known she was in trouble, we might have been able to help. At least we could have tried.

But as my due date approaches and the moment I've been anticipating nears, I feel confused, often overwhelmed by unexplained emotion that simmers right beneath the surface, threatening to erupt in tears. What's felt like an incredibly long and trying journey toward bringing a second child home is by all appearances about to end in the birth of a healthy baby, but loss is still wrapped up in that story, inextricable from the joy.

On a quiet Tuesday evening, I meet Jim and Sue Winkler at their home, a short drive from my own. I know of the Winklers through their son Brian, a former roommate of CJ's, and through Brian's wife Kim, whom I've gotten to know over playdates with our daughters, born just two months apart.

It's dark when I arrive, and Sue greets me at the door. We've met only once before, at a baby shower for Kim I hosted in our home about nine months ago, the same shower that was a difficult reminder of Avaleen's absence. In our interactions that night, I found Sue to be at peace with herself and adept at engaging others, and tonight she's equally as warm and gracious as she ushers me into the formal living room to meet Jim.

Both Jim and Sue are in their late seventies, closer in age to my grandparents than my parents. When Jim stands to shake my hand, I'm struck by the brightness of his eyes, and as we talk, his voice is clear and sharp. Sue has aged gracefully as well. Still tall and slim with blonde hair and luminous blue eyes, she looks a few decades younger than she is. From what Brian and Kim have told me, I know she regularly babysits many of her grandchildren and great-grandchildren and hosts weekly Sunday lunches for her large brood.

We converse briefly about my pregnancy while I take in my surroundings. The Winklers's living room carpet is white and spotless, vacuum lines visible. Above the couch where Jim and Sue sit are two charcoal prints, one of a sunflower and the other of apples on a branch, which I later learn Sue made when she was in high school.

Jim tells me that he first met Sue during their freshman year at a Catholic high school in their small Illinois town. They became friends, and Sue invited Jim to be her date for a hay ride at a friend's house. It was chilly that fall night, Jim remembers, and at one point, he asked Sue if her hands were cold. When she said they were, he suggested she put them in her pockets.

"Real romantic," Sue says, laughing.

"We were too young to really appreciate each other," adds Jim.

They remained friends, however, and during their senior year, when Sue was editor-in-chief of the school newspaper with Jim as her sports editor, their feelings blossomed. After Christmas of that year, they began dating.

When Jim moved to DC to attend Catholic University, everyone told Sue he would meet somebody else. They both agreed they could date other people, but each time Jim returned to Illinois on a break from school, they got together again. Eventually, they decided to get engaged. One week after

Jim's graduation from college and days after he received his commission in the Air Force, they were married. Sue was twenty-one; Jim had just turned twenty-two.

"I always say I didn't give him a chance to think about it," Sue says, laughing.

The Winklers both grew up in large Catholic families and attended twelve years of parochial school, so they saw faith in God as important. "It was pretty well engrained in us," Jim says. "I was a fervent believer."

They accepted the teachings of the Catholic Church about the value of children and chose not to use birth control, expecting they'd have a large family. When they were engaged, Sue remembers a conversation about how many children they'd like to have. She suggested four, but she recalls Jim, one of nine children himself, saying, "Oh, how about six?"

Their first child, a son named Jamie, came just eleven months after they were married, and another son, Danny, followed eighteen months later. During those early years, Jim and Sue lived first in Illinois, and then, as Jim pursued his Air Force career, in Florida and Texas and eventually New York. They were happy years, Sue recalls, filled with caring for their growing family and socializing with the many friends they'd made through the Air Force.

Two years after Danny was born, Jim accepted a job at the Naval Research Laboratory, and Jim and Sue moved their family to Northern Virginia. Jim, Sue, and their two young boys stayed at Jim's mother's house while they searched for a place of their own. Over the course of a few weeks, Sue began to experience minor abdominal pain, a pain she remembers as similar to menstrual cramping. At first, she didn't think much of it. Eventually, however, the pain became severe enough that she decided to go to the hospital.

Doctors there didn't know what was wrong, but after administering a test, they told her she was pregnant with her third child. After a few days in a hospital bed being treated with heat for the pain, Sue was ready to go home. It was almost Christmas, and she had two children waiting for her. Plus, no one could tell her exactly what was wrong.

"I think they suspected," Sue says. "[But] I guess they really didn't know what to do back then."

Her doctor didn't want her to leave the hospital and was "not pleased" when she did, Sue recalls, but she went home anyway, thinking her situation had improved and hoping it would resolve on its own.

One week later, however, she woke up early in the morning to go to the bathroom. When she lay back down in her bed, she realized she could no longer move. "It was like someone [had] plunged a sword into my abdomen," she says.

Jim was away in New York wrapping up business, so Sue called for her mother-in-law and sister-in-law, both of whom were in the home at the time. "I thought I was shouting for them," she says, "But they said they could barely hear me."

Thankfully, they did make out her voice and called an ambulance. "It was like a scene from one of those TV medical shows," Sue recalls. "They just ran. They put me on a cart and ran to the operating room and did immediate surgery."

When Sue awoke, she learned she'd been experiencing an ectopic pregnancy and was suffering from severe internal bleeding. The doctor told her that without surgery, she would have died within half an hour.

I think of how fortunate it was that she was in a home with other adults when she became paralyzed by her pain, and I imagine how differently things might have gone if she'd been home alone with her boys.

To save Sue's life, doctors had to remove the fetus along with one of Sue's Fallopian tubes. While she was in the recovery room, Jim, who'd finally arrived at the hospital, remembers the doctor bringing out the baby, still inside the Fallopian tube, for him to see. "I was just amazed," he says. He asked if there was anyone Catholic present who would be willing to baptize the baby, and a nurse said she would do it.

For Sue, the experience didn't cause much sadness. She was heavily sedated for several days after her surgery and remembers feeling confused. "I didn't expect anything like that to happen," she says.

Plus, since she'd only discovered she was pregnant after noticing troublesome symptoms, she'd never really had an opportunity to develop a connection with the baby. "It didn't seem real," she explains.

I've often wondered how I would've felt if I'd miscarried earlier, if news of death had come before news of new life had time to sink in. I imagine I would have been sad, but that the grief would have been different, perhaps less intense. Then again, I'm not sure. I think back to other women I've talked to, women like Christine and Sara, who felt their early losses deeply.

Neither Sue nor Jim remembers feeling particularly concerned about their ability to have more children, even though the removal of one Fallopian tube can reduce the monthly odds of a pregnancy by 50 percent.

Sue's doctors advised her to wait a full year before attempting another pregnancy, but four months later she was pregnant again. "Maybe we relaxed a little too much," she says, laughing.

Jim and Sue gave birth to a healthy daughter they named Pam and then twenty months later followed with a second daughter, Dianne. With four children ages six and under, their home was busy, and Sue often felt overwhelmed. When Dianne was only eight months old, Sue learned she was pregnant yet again. "I definitely did not want to get pregnant right away," she says, "so I wasn't very happy."

Two months into the pregnancy, Jim and Sue packed their pajama-clad crew into their station wagon and went to see *How the West Was Won* at the drive-in movie theater. In the middle of the movie, Jim recalls, Sue started bleeding.

"There was just no controlling it," she says.

They returned home and left their children in the care of Jim's mother. Jim called Sue's obstetrician, who had been up most of the night delivering babies and said he could probably see Sue the next morning. "I'm taking her to the hospital," Jim remembers telling the doctor, "and you better be there when I get there."

"And he was," Sue says.

The doctor tried to temper the bleeding with Vitamin K shots but were unable to stop it.

Later, after the miscarriage was complete, Sue struggled with guilt. She worried she'd somehow caused the miscarriage by picking up two-year-old Pam earlier the same day the bleeding started. "I felt like something tore loose," she says, remembering that moment.

I recall struggling with similar feelings of guilt in the weeks after Avaleen died. I'd been very careful about my caffeine intake throughout my pregnancy, but days before we learned she was gone, I'd permitted myself two small cups of caffeinated iced tea at a friend's barbeque. No matter how often CJ and my doctor told me that wouldn't have caused a miscarriage, I felt uncertain. *What if it had?* I wondered. *How could they know it wasn't somehow my fault?*

Sue also felt guilty about not immediately embracing her pregnancy. She thought, just as Christopher and Mary Grace had, that perhaps God was punishing her for not desiring the baby. "I felt like God said, 'Okay, then I won't give you a baby. You don't want to be pregnant.'"

While she was in the hospital, her doctor took her by the hand and told her the miscarriage wasn't her fault. He explained it might have been caused by some sort of "imperfection" in the baby. "He was trying to make me feel better," Sue says.

Still, she battled deep sadness for months. "I cried a lot," she remembers. "I know that I was depressed, but I had a pretty large family to care for. We were busy; that kind of helps you get through it."

I can understand. The need to take care of Ellie was what got me out of bed on many of those early days after Avaleen died. She needed me, and I needed to be needed, to be pulled out of myself and into the healing rhythms of normal life: diapers to be changed, meals to be prepared, playgrounds and pools to be visited. At the same time, Ellie's constant neediness also made it difficult for me to find space to grieve, to have the necessary solitary moments to engage the pain and wade through it. I can only imagine what the experience would have been like if I'd had four small children like Sue did at the time of her miscarriage, how little room for grief there must have been.

About a year later, while dealing with ongoing sorrow and continued busyness, Sue learned she was pregnant yet again. "I think that just added to your depression," Jim says, looking at Sue.

She agrees, describing the experience of that pregnancy and the years that followed the birth of another son, Chris, as a "crisis of faith." While she continued attending church and praying with her children, she says, she felt burdened.

"Sue felt like she wasn't able to pursue her talents," Jim explains. She liked to paint and had taken courses in high school but had no time for artistic endeavors in her hectic life as a mother of five small children.

"I could tell where she was coming from," Jim continues. "She had talents and yet she wasn't able to express them because she was taking care of kids all the time."

"Well the sixties were difficult times," Sue explains. "Vietnam and free love ... and women's lib ... I liked staying home with the children, but I did feel like I wanted to fulfill myself, find myself or something."

"How do you look back on that now?" I ask. We're a half-century removed from the sixties, but I can relate to the tension she's describing. We're still asking the same questions today, wondering how to hold motherhood in balance with our interests and talents and careers.

"I think it's kind of silly now," she says. "I wish I had turned to God instead of yoga and other pursuits."

At the time, however, what Sue was feeling was anything but silly. Jim remembers multiple evenings when the kids were all sleeping and Sue would simply sit and cry. "I didn't know what to do for her," he says. "I kind of shut down, and I didn't see any solution to the problem, so I didn't really offer anything. In that respect, I guess I failed her."

"No," Sue replies immediately. She's told me earlier that she sees Jim as a source of stability, that she doesn't know what she'd do without him.

"Well, at least I wasn't smart enough to come up with the right answers," Jim insists.

I'm impressed with his humility and transparency. It's not easy, I know, for most men to stay engaged with a problem they can't solve. It's even harder for most men to admit failing the wives they love.

Sue doesn't see it that way, however. "I didn't always open my heart to him or anyone else," she says. "I would just say, 'No, everything's fine.'"

She attributes her crisis of faith primarily to the unrelenting demands of caring for multiple small children, but I keep thinking about the miscarriage that seemed to spark her sadness. "Do you think the unresolved grief of the miscarriage was part of the crisis?" I ask.

"Probably," Sue says. "[Kids are] cute and they make you laugh . . . but you still have to have time to get over certain things."

At the height of her desperation, when Chris was nearly two years old, Sue remembers a particular moment of prayer. "I remember crying out to God and saying, 'Don't you care?'" she says. "I just felt like, *Is this all there is?*"

Shortly after that prayer, Sue received a call from a neighbor inviting her to a women's retreat and decided to attend. "Everything that was said on that retreat was directed to my heart," she remembers. "I felt like I really found Jesus there."

Sue had a strong sense that Jesus was speaking right to her, communicating how much He loved her. For a long time, she says, "I had felt that no one knew what I was going through."

Her experience on the retreat changed that, and her crisis of faith lifted.

But neither Jim nor Sue was sure they wanted more children. Before Chris's birth, they'd followed the teaching of the Catholic Church regarding contraception. "We always figured God would give us the number [of] children He wanted us to have," Jim says.

But with five small children already, they decided to try the pill. Sue spoke with a priest who told her it would be okay. "In the Church, you could get just about any answer you wanted depending on what priest you went to," Jim explains.

"Especially if you had five children," Sue clarifies.

Nine years passed with no more pregnancies, and despite Chris's persistent prayers for a younger brother, Jim and Sue believed their family was complete. However, in Sue's late thirties, motivated in part by concerns about the ethics of the pill and in part by a sense that her age had made her less fertile, she stopped taking it, relying instead on Natural Family Planning.

A few years later, at age thirty-nine, she found herself pregnant one more time. "We were both shocked," Sue says. "Jim found it easier to accept than I did."

Jim remembers his co-workers expressing disbelief when he told them that he and Sue were expecting another child. One co-worker in particular, who believed the world was already overpopulated, saw Jim and Sue's large family as irresponsible.

"I guess there are some cases where that's true," Jim says. "But . . . we consider children a blessing, and we would always take care of them."

"You can't think of it as a mistake when you look back," Sue says. "You love each one so much."

A fourth son, Brian, was born just before her fortieth birthday.

I don't come from a large family, but I can relate to what they're saying. My own mother experienced two difficult pregnancies with my brother and me, so my youngest brother was an unplanned "surprise." Now, however, it's impossible to imagine our family without him, without the humor and energy and happiness he's brought us all.

"I look back over our life, and I can see how God guided us," Sue says. "God is good. We've been through a lot, but we've always been blessed."

"We still feel like God was always taking care of us," Jim adds, "whether we were conscious of it at the time or not."

I've asked all the questions on my list, and Jim excuses himself for a moment. I realize I have one more question for Sue. I want to know if after fifty years, near the end of a good and full life, the children Sue and Jim lost still matter to them as much as they once did, or if they've faded into distant memory with time. Searching for the right words, I ask, "Do you think at all about meeting your babies?"

Sue tells me she does imagine meeting her children in heaven one day. "More and more as I get older," she says. "I don't think I thought about it too much when I was younger because I was just busy."

It comforts me to hear her say this, to think that in a way, the babies she's lost have become even closer to her heart over the years. I've often feared that the passage of time and the birth of another child will cause me to lose Avaleen, that the space in my heart that used to be hers will be filled with other things. Certainly, having a second child to care for will make my days busier, and there will be even less time for the reflection that feels essential to carrying on her memory.

But Sue's words give me permission for this, for the exhausting reality of raising small children, for the consuming work that will at times make me think less about Avaleen. They remind me that this experience—like the deep, dark days of early grief—will be a phase, and it too will be temporary.

Perhaps, I think, what I'm feeling is what all parents feel when they're about to add another child to their family, the growing pains of a heart being stretched beyond its current capacity, the fear there won't be enough love to go around.

A few weeks ago, two dear friends gave me a necklace as a baby present. It's a simple silver chain with four circles, a large one to represent me and three small ones to represent my three girls: the two year old I care for every day, the baby I never got to hold, and this little one we get to meet next week.

It's a beautiful, thoughtful gift, and I cried putting it on for the first time, so grateful that my friends chose to acknowledge the lives of all three of my precious girls. I love wearing it, love running my fingers over the three tiny circles and thinking about each of my three children, about how I know and love each of them in such different ways.

I don't know what I'm supposed to feel at a moment like this. I'm not even sure exactly what I'm feeling. But I do know that God has given me three girls, that each of their lives has been a gift, that I'm blessed to be their mother and to carry them as I do right now: in my arms, in my womb, and in my heart.

—BLOG POST, NOVEMBER 24, 2013

Chapter 15

DECEMBER

It's dark when the alarm clock sounds the morning of November 26. I've slept fitfully the past few hours, but when I hear the jarring beeps, I'm wide awake. *Today's the day,* I think. *It's finally here.*

We planned to try for a vaginal delivery, but just a few weeks ago, I learned I'd be required to have a scheduled C-section instead, thanks to a T-incision the doctor delivering Ellie needed to make. Wanting to minimize my risk of uterine rupture, we scheduled the C-section for today, six days before my due date and two days before Thanksgiving.

The house is quiet while we shower and load our bags into the car. Ellie and CJ's parents, who are here to watch her while we're gone, are still asleep. Our drive to the hospital is quiet and black, which seems somehow fitting. On the day of Ellie's birth, we also drove to the hospital during pre-dawn hours. I was nervous then too, worried I wouldn't be able to handle the pain and concerned about all the unknowns of the days and weeks to follow. This time, I know much of what's coming: the way I'll be separated from CJ while they prep me for surgery; the strange sensations of a needle plunging into my spine and my numbed stomach being pulled open; the piercing, beautiful sound of a first cry.

I've thought a lot about the moment of first meeting this baby, of what it will feel like to finally hold a newborn in my arms again. I've wondered if it will be magical and healing and redemptive. I've wondered if I will weep, overcome with joy and relief, the way a character in a movie might at such a climactic moment.

But lying on the hospital bed in pre-op, attached to heart-rate monitors and an IV, I can't stop shaking. For months, I've longed for this exact moment, and now, I wish I were anywhere but here. With Ellie, I hadn't had to wait like this for the C-section to begin. By the time the doctor decided it would be necessary, they'd wheeled me straight into the operating room and prepped me immediately. Then, the only emotion I remember feeling was relief that after fourteen hours of Pitocin-induced contractions without pain medication, I'd get to meet my baby soon.

This time, though, there's time to think. Too much time. "Are you all right?" CJ asks, his eyes searching mine.

"No," I say. "I'm really nervous."

"It's going to be okay," he says, like he always does.

You don't know that, I think, like I always do.

C-sections are a routine surgery and the risk of complications is low. Many babies are delivered this way, and I've already survived and recovered from one without incident. I also trust my doctor completely. But it would be a lie to say I didn't feel terrified. A C-section is still a major surgery, and there's always a chance something could go dreadfully wrong. Plus, I'm well aware that statistics are no guarantee. Women still die giving birth in America.

Avaleen died when the odds were in her favor, I think. *So could I.*

"If anything happens to me," I ask CJ, "will you tell Ellie how much I love her?"

"Nothing is going to happen to you," he says.

In the operating room, my doctor holds my hand while the anesthesiologist administers a spinal block. With that step out of the way, CJ is allowed to join me, and he takes his place seated by my head while the operation begins. In just moments, I hear loud screams, and my doctor holds up our daughter. With her tiny blood-covered fingers, she grabs onto the drape that obstructed my view of the surgery, and the room fills with laughter. "I've never seen a baby do that before," somebody says.

"She's beautiful," my doctor tells us.

And she is. CJ holds her face close to mine while they finish stitching me up, and I try to take it all in—the fact that she's truly, finally here, that she's healthy and beautiful and very much alive.

I feel joy and relief, but I don't cry or want to cry. Instead, I feel a rather ordinary peace. I listen to my doctor and her surgical assistant chat casually while they stitch me back together, and I whisper comforting words to my little girl as CJ holds her, longing for the moment I can hold her myself.

We name her Celia Joy. Celia means *heavenly*, and we like the meaning of her names together, the idea of heavenly joy. When she was growing inside me, we prayed she would be a fighter, able to handle whatever my body might throw at her. We hope that as she matures, she'll remain a fighter for heavenly joy in her own heart and in the hearts of others, and we hope too that her life will be a source of joy from heaven for our family.

And from the earliest moments, it is. During our stay in the hospital, CJ and I keep commenting about how different Celia is from how Ellie was as a newborn, how much more easily nursing comes to her, how content she is. At home, she's happy to sit in her bouncy seat and watch her big sister play, and she quickly begins sleeping eight to twelve hour stretches overnight. When she cries, it's generally because she's tired or hungry, problems I can understand and easily fix. Ellie adores her and quickly adjusts to her role as a big sister.

To be sure, there are difficult moments in those early days: swollen, throbbing breasts or times I'd like to pay attention to Ellie and can't. But, overwhelmingly, Celia's life is a source of much happiness for all of us. Even on the worst days, I can't forget how much of a treasure she is, how grateful I am that even when she's fussy and needy, she is, quite simply, *here*.

I sit in the glider in my bedroom on a warm December morning, sunshine filling the room in spite of the closed blinds. Ellie is happily playing with my mom downstairs, and I rock a sleeping Celia. Her small body is snuggled warm against my chest, her breathing deep and steady, and I press my lips to the top of her head, savoring the bliss of holding her close.

I think of Avaleen, of the fact that I never had this moment with her, that she'd never known the comfort of being held in my arms.

There is great joy here, and there is great sadness. Once, I thought the sadness would forever drown out the joy, but now I realize that grieving Avaleen has created space for them both.

I hold my newborn daughter as silent tears slide down my cheeks.

Epilogue

It's been over three years now since we lost Avaleen. It's hard for me to remember what life was like before her, when I'd never tasted real grief or been forced to confront the terrible realities of death. Even though we never met her, she's part of our story now, woven into our lives in ways I never could have anticipated. I think of her when I see a mother with three daughters at Starbucks, when I meet a three-year-old girl, when I remember a party CJ and I attended while she was still alive inside me.

A year and a half ago, we told Ellie about her second sister, and she's felt her loss more deeply than we expected. Most days, she talks about Avaleen, announcing to friends and strangers that there are three kids in our family. She asks questions about heaven and death and tells me regularly that she misses Avaleen, that she wants us all to die so we can go to heaven and be with her. "I understand," I tell her. And yet I'm surprised by how readily she's embraced the sister she never met, how instinctively she holds Avaleen's life close to her heart.

I'm surprised, too, by the way I continue to carry the stories of the eleven families in this book. I struggle to see God in the daily chaos of two little ones, and I remember Sue's crisis of faith and take comfort in how God met her. I hear news of a friend's stillbirth, and I remember what Mark said about his friend who "just showed up." I think about the terrifying uncertainties of expanding our family further, and I return to a point Jared made—that avoiding risk is a risk in itself. I expected to be encouraged by the couples I talked to. What I didn't expect was the ways in which their words became part of my consciousness and my own ongoing story.

I find also that I'm deeply invested in the continuing stories of these families. I grieved reading Sara Brode's blog updates following our interview, learning that after her long journey to a specialist, still month after month passed without a pregnancy. I understood when she and Justin eventually decided to stop trying for another child, but I ached for them too. *Why God?* I questioned. *I don't understand.*

When the Erb family was finally able to make their adoption of Davison official, I was ecstatic as I clicked through the Facebook photos and witnessed the family's joy. I celebrated, too, in finding out that Kim was pregnant again and that she'd made it well past the point of her earlier losses. *What a beautiful, unexpected blessing,* I thought. But my heart broke when, at their nineteen-week ultrasound, Jared and Kim learned their unborn son had a fatal condition called bronchial atresia. Caedmon Ezekiel was delivered via C-section at thirty-one weeks, and his family had one brief hour to love and hold him before he died. About a month later, their foster daughter Kyla, whom they'd hoped to adopt, also left their home.

In what Kim describes as a "glimpse of joy after a night of sorrow," she and Jared were able to adopt Jayden on Caedmon's original due date. At that point, they decided their family was complete. But I recently received an e-mail from Kim. The Erbs have decided to take in the newborn biological sister of their adopted sons and should be able to adopt her soon. Jared is also about to release a CD of children's music titled *Things Above* in honor of Caedmon. In her e-mail to me, Kim quotes Ps 126:6: "*He who goes out weeping . . . shall come home with shouts of joy.*"

Alex and Amanda Robertson's story has also been marked by emotional highs and lows. In the months following our interview, they had two more miscarriages, both little girls at around ten weeks. Then, after learning they were expecting twins, they lost one of the babies early in the pregnancy. The other, a daughter they named Adeline, was recently born full-term, healthy and strong. When I finally hear this report from Amanda over the phone, I breathe a deep sigh of relief. I know they have more embryos they plan to implant, but I hope they've turned a corner, that doctors have finally figured out the cocktail of medications that will help them avoid more loss.

There has been other happy news too. Scott and Christine added a healthy baby boy named Daniel to their family. Mary Grace Peters, who'd been told her whole life that she wasn't athletic, ran her first half-marathon this past fall. Dave and Cathy Bowman have relocated to Atlanta, Georgia to participate in a growing Navigators ministry to at-risk youth, college students, and local churches throughout the city. Joshua Anderson will soon finish his master's degree in human service counseling, and Bethany has returned to school at well, where she's completing an undergraduate degree in medical biology with plans to enroll in medical school in the next few years. She hopes to become a pediatrician serving at-risk kids both in the United States and around the world.

CJ and I would like to have another child. I'm currently fourteen weeks pregnant with a baby who, should everything go well, will be born around the time this book is released. But just this month, a close friend experienced her second consecutive second-trimester loss, and I'm freshly aware of life's uncertainty.

I continue to wrestle with God. I still don't understand why Avaleen had to die. Some days, I try to, wading my way through Tim Keller's thick tome, *Walking with God through Pain and Suffering.* I grapple with terms like *theodicy* and *immanent frame* and feel reassured that there are smart people who can reconcile a belief in God with life's horrors. I think about what I read, about the inability of our modern, Western culture to make meaning of pain, about the beauty of a God unlike any other, a God who is both sovereign and suffering. Often, though, I find myself wondering, *Can it really be? Can I keep on believing in a good and loving God? Can I orient my whole life around following Him? Could I possibly have it all wrong?*

It feels that way sometimes, when I try to explain life and death and God and heaven to Ellie, who's now four. "Is it real?" she asks, and I can't blame her. It is the stuff of fairy tales—God born as a baby, the dead raised to life, a future of eternal bliss. It can seem too good and too simple to be true.

But when I think about my own life and about the stories of the families in this book, I can't help but see glimpses of God in the darkness, of blessings that flow "far as the curse is found."[18] And I can't help but whisper, borrowing the words of one of Scripture's grieving parents: *I do believe; help my unbelief.*[19]

18. Watts, "Joy to the World," line 13.
19. Mark 9:24 (NASB).

Acknowledgments

From the beginning, this book has been something I felt God called me to do, but like most callings fulfilled, it has been far from a solo effort.

CJ, you eagerly embraced this book the day I first mentioned it and have never once looked back. You've cheerfully offered countless evening and weekend hours to be the primary parent while I wrote and have walked with me through every challenge, setback, and triumph along the way. I'm deeply grateful for your steady, faithful love and for the fact that we get to experience sickness and health, joy and sorrow together. I love you.

Ellie and Celia, your beautiful lives are a sweeter gift that you will ever know. I always knew I wanted to be a mommy, but watching you grow day by day has been a greater privilege than I ever imagined. Thank you for "sharing me" while I wrote this book and for running eagerly into my arms every time I came home.

Mom and Dad, you knew even before I did that I was a writer, and in so many ways, it is because of you that this book exists. Thank you for showing me what it looks like to love Jesus even when it's hard, for teaching me to write and encouraging all of my early, faltering efforts, and for your ongoing sacrificial love expressed in meals made, grandchildren cared for, laundry folded, and prayers faithfully prayed.

Charlie and Dianna, you've graciously welcomed me into your family and given generously of your time to care for all of us. You are always willing and eager to serve in any way we ask. This book would not have been possible without your help.

Joel and Jen, Nate and Ashley, thank you for the ways you've entered in to my pain in losing Avaleen and in to the process of writing this book. I love you all.

Connally, thank you for helping me discover my inner artist and for faithfully investing in my life these past thirteen years. You know me so well, and God regularly uses your words to minister to the deep places in my soul.

Becca, Randi, Linda, Star, Rachel, Shannon, Megan, Joanna, Bonnie, Marcy, Melinda, and the other ladies in my wonderful small group, thank you for walking with me in the darkness and for your compassionate care for my heart. I love you all.

Liz and Jess, I'm very thankful for our years together teaching middle school and the friendships that have continued far beyond. You are both faithful, generous, excellent friends.

Heidi and Kellie, thank you for understanding what Avaleen means to me and for willingly and creatively entering into my hectic life as a mom. I'm very blessed to have friends like you.

Hannah, Linda, Rachel, Paige, and Randi, thank you for caring for our girls so well while I wrote this book. We all think you are the greatest.

Jess, Cortney, Rachel, Star, Heidi, Steph, Josh, and Sarah, thank you for generously giving your time and for providing helpful feedback on drafts of this book.

Bethanie, Christine, Pam, Lisa, and Bonnie, thank you for reading with your own hearts and stories in view and for helping me see the book through your eyes.

Dr. W, thank you for reviewing the sections of the draft containing medical information and, more importantly, for the excellent care you've extended to our entire family during each of my pregnancies.

Kirsten, thank you for engaging so deeply with this project and for guiding me through the revision and editing processes. I'm incredibly thankful for your deep heart, your attention to detail, and the love you bring to all of your work. This book is so much better because of you.

My friends and family too numerous to name who have prayed for me over the past the three years as I've written this book, thank you for reading my updates and asking how things were going and most of all for bringing this book before God in prayer.

The families whose stories are the heart of this book, thank you for inviting me into your homes and bravely sharing so much of yourselves with me and with the readers of these pages. You all are among the most brave and beautiful people I know, and I continue to be inspired by your lives.

And finally, Jesus, I've loved you since I was a little girl, and I love you still. Thank you for loving me at my messiest and ugliest and for calling me your daughter.

Appendix

Resources That Helped Me

What follows is by no means an exhaustive list of resources. Rather, it's a collection of a few books, articles, and websites I found helpful at various points in my journey.

RESOURCES FOR INFERTILITY

I couldn't find much to read when we struggled to get pregnant, but I wish I'd discovered these resources back then.

- "The Gift of Infertility" by Miroslav Volf, *Christian Century*, June 14, 2005.
  This is the article Brian Johnson referenced and later sent to me.

- *Every Bitter Thing is Sweet* by Sara Hagerty, Zondervan, 2014.
  I loved this beautiful, moving memoir of how God showed up in one woman's pain, including her experience of infertility.

- The Carry Camp, www.thecarrycamp.com.
  This organization focuses on caring for women dealing with infertility, offering blog posts as well as retreats.

- RESOLVE: The National Infertility Association, www.resolve.org.
  This organization's website is filled with extensive resources for couples dealing with infertility.

RESOURCES FOR EARLY GRIEF

When I first lost Avaleen, all I wanted to read, and all I could really handle reading, were stories. Here are a few I found helpful:

- *About What Was Lost: Twenty Writers on Miscarriage, Stillbirth, and Infant Death* edited by Jessica Berger Gross, Plume, 2006.
  While this compilation of essays does not address questions of faith specifically, I found it worthwhile to read multiple perspectives on loss.

- Still Standing Magazine, stillstandingmag.com.
  This web magazine regularly publishes helpful articles about infertility and child loss.

- *Rare Bird* by Anna Whiston-Donaldson, Convergent, 2014.
  This beautiful memoir recounts the sudden, tragic death of the author's twelve-year-old son and the questions about God and faith she processes as she grieves.

RESOURCES FOR LATER

When the consuming grief subsided, I was able to benefit from books of a more intellectual and theological nature. Here are a few I liked:

- *Hope Deferred: Heart-Healing Reflections on Reproductive Loss* edited by Nadine Pence Frantz and Mary T. Stimming, Wipf & Stock, 2010.
  This book is written by four female theologians with diverse denominational perspectives and is both personal and academic in its exploration of loss.

- *What Was Lost: A Christian Journey Through Miscarriage* by Elise Erickson Barrett, Westminster John Knox, 2010.
  Written by a United Methodist pastor who has experienced miscarriage herself, this book provides valuable insights on the grief process and reconnecting with God after loss.

- *Naming the Child: Hope-filled Reflections on Miscarriage, Stillbirth, and Infant Death* by Jenny Schroedel, Paraclete, 2009.
  The author is Christian, but the text is only vaguely so. Still, it provides helpful reflections on grief, particularly for those who've lost children late in pregnancy or shortly after birth.

- *Walking with God Through Pain and Suffering* by Tim Keller, Riverhead, 2015.
  I gained much from Keller's thoughtful exploration of suffering through a philosophical-theological lens.

PRACTICAL RESOURCES:

I was also helped along the way by several practical resources including:

- *Taking Charge of Your Fertility* by Toni Weschler, William Morrow, 2015.
  I read this book soon after we started trying to get pregnant and found it to be a good starting point for understanding my body and optimizing our chances for a pregnancy.

- *Avoiding Miscarriage: Everything You Need to Know To Feel More Confident In Pregnancy* by Susan Rousselot, Sea Change, 2006.
  Reading this book helped me comprehend the various causes of miscarriage and what tests and treatments I should consider moving forward.

- Sara Brode's Repro Renegade blog, now hosted at survivingrecurrentmiscarriage.wordpress.com.
  This is a great place to start if you're interested in learning more about Sara's story or about the growing field of reproductive immunology, which has been helpful for many people.

Bibliography

Altrogge, Mark. "In the Presence." http://www.guitaretab.com/m/mark-altrogge/376900. html.

The American College of Obstetricians and Gynecologists. "Early Pregnancy Loss." http://www.acog.org/~/media/For%20Patients/faq090.pdf.

Baird, Meghan, et al. "Behold Our God (Who Has Held the Oceans)." http://sovereigngracemusic.org/Songs/Behold_Our_God_(Who_has_held_the_oceans)/1.

ESV Study Bible. Wheaton, IL: Crossway, 2008.

Flowers, Lois. *Infertility: Finding God's Peace in the Journey*. Eugene, OR: Harvest House, 2003.

Lotz, Ann Graham. *Why?: Trusting God When You Don't Understand*. Nashville, TN: Thomas Nelson, 2005.

Oakley, Paul. "Jesus, Lover of My Soul (It's All About You)." http://www.worshiptogether.com/songs/jesus-lover-of-my-soul-its-all-about-you/.

RESOLVE: The National Infertility Association. "Myth about Secondary Infertility." http://www.resolve.org/about-infertility/medical-conditions/myth-about-secondary-infertility.html.

———. "Myths and Facts About Infertility." http://www.resolve.org/support/for-family--friends/myths-and-facts.html.

Schroedel, Jenny. *Naming the Child: Hope-filled Reflections on Miscarriage, Stillbirth, and Infant Death*. Brewster, MA: Paraclete, 2009.

Volf, Miroslav. "The Gift of Infertility." *Christian Century* 122, no. 12 (June 14, 2005), 33.

Von Schlegel, Katharina. "Be Still, My Soul." http://www.lutheranhymnal.com/lyrics/lw510.htm.

Watts, Isaac. "Joy to the World! The Lord Is Come." http://www.hymnary.org/text/joy_to_the_world_the_lord_is_come.